A B C

FOR

BOOK COLLECTORS

BY

JOHN CARTER

RUPERT HART-DAVIS
LONDON

[TITLE-PAGE]

First published September 1952
Second edition, revised, 1953
Third edition, revised, 1961
Fourth edition, revised, 1966
Reprinted, with corrections, 1967
Reprinted, 1971
Fifth edition, revised, 1972

Printed in Great Britain by
Fletcher & Son Ltd, Norwich

[PRINTER'S IMPRINT]

TO
JOHN HAYWARD
R.I.P.

PREFACE

EVERY specialised profession or pursuit develops its own jargon, much of which is unintelligible to the layman. How many general readers can give the meaning of *nisi prius, bareboat charter, baton cut, piecrust border, forced rouge, deleted vocals, an equated A6, slightly ullaged* or *high-factor backward paragraph loops?*[1] Book-collecting is no exception; and although a good many of its specialised terms are defined in such broader works as G. A. Glaister's *Glossary of the Book* (1960), while others are explained in the more elementary manuals for collectors, no attempt, so far as I know, has been made to deal comprehensively with the terminology of this particular subject and no other, between one pair of covers. The present book is the result of such an attempt, undertaken in response to an observation made to me years ago by a friend (not a book collector), who said that although he always read the back page of *The Times Literary Supplement* before the rest of the paper, he was tired of encountering there terms inadequately defined in the dictionaries.

My objective, then, has been to isolate and to define, and sometimes to comment upon, such words and phrases, commonly used in book-collecting, as would be likely to puzzle an educated reader faced for the first time by a bookseller's or an auctioneer's catalogue. Most of these are, of course, tolerably well understood by collectors; and they have come to be used by professionals with the unthinking familiarity of Pitman or Gregg to a shorthand typist. But with the passage of time (and book-collecting is an ancient pursuit) our private language has become heavily encrusted with technical terms, special meanings for ordinary words, and jargon of various kinds. Many such terms are borrowed from the language of bibliography, others from that

[1] The Law, shipping, precious stones, furniture, Eton football, gramophone records, the Foreign Office, wine, figure-skating.

of printers, paper-makers, binders or publishers. But to both groups collectors, and the booksellers who serve them, have often given their own glosses and specialised connotations. There are also many words and phrases native to the antiquarian book-market but Greek to anyone outside it.

This is not an encyclopædia. It is an ABC. And it is not an ABC of bibliography, or of printing or binding or book-production terms, though many of these come into it. It is an ABC of book-*collecting*, for novices, would-be collectors and that section of the literate public which takes an interest in our pursuit without necessarily wishing to share it. If it were also of service to antiquarian booksellers' younger assistants—and, after all, even a Bernard Quaritch or a Karl Hiersemann has to start somewhere—it would be no more than a small repayment for the professional brains I myself have been picking for a quarter of a century.

One or two points need a special word of explanation. Latin and French terms have been included only when they are in common use or have no satisfactory or accepted English equivalent. The language of binding, for instance, is liberally sprinkled with French words; and though we may think that most of these could have been englished by now if the experts had not rather a liking for them, the fact is that many of them never have been. Reference books and bibliographies have been excluded, except those few (e.g. STC, Hain, McKerrow, Wing) which are such household words to cataloguers that they are constantly cited without any clue to their scope or nature. Entries dealing with printers, presses, publishers, binders and the like have been reduced to the minimum, since once started on these there would be no stopping. The meaning of certain words commonly used by cataloguers has been assumed to be self-evident: e.g. as new, clean, faded, frayed, stained, browned, broken, worn, polished, refurbished, rust-hole, alignment. And where a word like *anonymous* seemed to call for a note, I have not insulted the reader's intelligence by first defining it.

Finally, it must be clearly understood that this is a sadly

8

insular book. The taste,[1] technique and terminology of book-collecting on the Continent differ in so many respects from those of Great Britain and the U.S.A. that it seemed better to exclude continental usage altogether than to make an ineffectual attempt at meeting the widely different needs of those collectors who read foreign booksellers' catalogues without knowing the language.[2] Moreover, although English and American collectors speak much the same language, it must be further understood that where I have made statements or offered dates or risked generalisations about the history of book production or distribution, I am referring to English practice only.

The arrangement of entries is alphabetical, but groups of cognate terms have sometimes been combined under a single entry; many adjectives of condition, for instance, are dealt with under the general article. Abbreviations are grouped together at the beginning, but most of the terms they represent appear in the main alphabet in their expanded form. Cross-reference is effected (sparingly and with plenty of apparent inconsistencies) by the use of SMALL CAPITALS; so that when, for example, in the article on *Collation*, there is mention of CANCELS, the reader who does not know what a cancel is can turn to the separate entry; while the reader of the entry on *Colonial Editions* who comes across a reference to PUBLISHER'S CLOTH is similarly directed from the particular to the general.

Although, as a professional, I can hardly be expected to avoid some bias, I have tried to be impartial in those matters where buyer and seller do not always see eye to eye. It would be too much to hope that I have succeeded, in a

[1] In respect of French bibliophily Ernest Hemingway recorded the following conversation with an old lady in charge of a second-hand bookstall in Paris:

Q. 'How do you tell valuable French books?'

A. 'First there are the pictures. Then it is a question of the quality of the pictures. Then it is the binding. If a book is good, the owner will have it bound properly. All books in English are bound, but bound badly. There is no way of judging them.'

[2] *Dictionary for the Antiquarian Book-trade*, in eight languages, edited by Menno Hertzberger, is published by the International League of Antiquarian Booksellers.

9

book from which I have not attempted to exclude my own opinions. But I was not displeased to find that, among the friends who scrutinised the first draft, it was a bookseller who thought I had been disrespectful to the book-trade, a collector who considered my approach to collecting aggressively commercial, and an ex-employee of a famous auction house who thought I had been unfair to auctioneers. These reactions suggested that my prejudices, however regrettable, were at least evenly distributed.

It was obvious from the start that an undertaking of this kind must depend heavily on the assistance of friendly experts. My publishers (and in particular Mr. Richard Garnett) have given me not only encouragement but much practical advice. My wife, Sir Dennis Proctor, and Sir Edward Playfair (to please whom the book was begun) acted as lay assessors, and under this battery of studied innocence the first draft was drastically purged of jargon and obscurities. Mr. Howard Nixon made extensive contribution to the entries dealing with leather binding, a difficult and specialised subject with which I found myself painfully ill-equipped to grapple. Mr. Brooke Crutchley refined the entries concerned with the technique of printing and paper-making. Messrs. Dudley Massey, Percy Muir, Arnold Muirhead, A. N. L. Munby, Simon Nowell-Smith, Graham Pollard, John Sparrow and the late Michael Sadleir, whom I think of as a sort of Tenth Legion, found time in the midst of busy lives to scrutinise and correct the whole work in draft; and there is hardly a paragraph which does not bear traces of their help.

To all these I offer my heartfelt thanks. To one other old friend, who fostered this project in its infancy and laboured unsparingly in its development, my indebtedness is such that the least I could do was to give his name a page to itself.

NOTE TO THE FIFTH EDITION

W HEN I was first at work on this manual Stanley Morison observed that it sounded like the sort of book which might be a serviceable thing by the time it reached its fifth edition. Well, twenty years later, thanks to the kindness of the public and the confidence of my publishers, it now has. Previous revisions have owed much, like the original book, to the assistance of observant readers—in some cases strangers from far corners—and this present edition, which is more substantially revised than has been practicable since the third (of 1961) owes notable debts to Mr. Howard Nixon (not for the first time), Professor G. Thomas Tanselle, Mr. T. B. Belanger, Mr. George Painter, Mr. Anthony Hobson, and in particular to Dr. Philip Gaskell, whose *A New Introduction to Bibliography* is designed to do for our generation what McKerrow (so often cited in the following pages) did for that of 1927.

Chelsea
St. Andrew's Day 1971

[PRELIMINARY LEAVES *end here*]

ABC FOR BOOK COLLECTORS

ABBREVIATIONS

The prevalence of these in booksellers' catalogues varies with the descriptive formula. An elaborate catalogue will have few, but most cataloguers use the familiar ones, and in short-title or clearance lists there may be a good many—sometimes explained at the beginning, more often not.

Even the abbreviations in common use are not all wholly standardised, nor does the following list pretend to be exhaustive. Most of its contents appear, under the expanded term, in the main alphabet: to those which do not, page references have been appended where appropriate.

ABA	Antiquarian Booksellers' Association.
ABAA	Antiquarian Booksellers' Association of America.
ABPC	American Book-prices Current.
A.D.	Autograph document.
A.D.s.	Autograph document, signed.
Ads., advts., adverts.	Advertisements.
A.e.g.	All edges gilt.
A.L.	Autograph letter, not signed.
A.L.s.	Autograph letter, signed.
A.Ms.s	Autograph manuscript, signed.
A.N.s.	Autograph note, signed.
BAR	Book Auction Records.
Bd.	Bound.
Bdg.	Binding.
Bds.	Boards.
B.L.	Black letter.
BMC	British Museum Catalogue.
BPC	Book Prices Current.
C., *ca.*	*Circa* (about, approximately).
C. & p.	Collated and perfect.
Cat.	Catalogue.

CBEL	. .	Cambridge Bibliography of English Literature.
Cent.	. .	Century.
Cf.	. .	Calf.
Cl.	. .	Cloth.
Col(d).	. .	Colour(ed).
Cont.	. .	Contemporary.
Cr. 8vo	. .	Crown octavo (p. 101).
Dec.	. .	Decorated.
Doc.	. .	Document (p. 33).
D-j., d-w.	.	Dust-jacket, dust-wrapper.
DNB	. .	Dictionary of National Biography.
Ed.	. .	Edition, editor, edited.
E.D.L.	. .	Edition de luxe.
Endp., e.p.	.	Endpaper(s).
Eng., engr.	.	Engraved, engraving(s).
Ex-lib.	. .	Ex-library.
Facs.	. .	Facsimile.
Fcp.	. .	Foolscap (p. 101).
F., ff.	. .	Folio, folios (i.e. leaves).
Fo., fol.	.	Folio, a size of book.
Fp., front.	.	Frontispiece.
G., gt.	. .	Gilt.
G.e.	. .	Gilt edges.
GKW, GW	.	Gesamtkatalog der Wiegendrucke.
G.L.	. .	Gothic letter.
G.t.	. .	Gilt tops
Hf.	. .	Half (e.g. hf.cf. = half calf).
Hf. bd.	. .	Half bound.
ILAB	. .	International League of Antiquarian Booksellers.
Ill., ills.	. .	Illustrated, illustrations.
Imp.	. .	Imperial.
Impft.	. .	Imperfect.
Inscr.	. .	Inscribed, inscription.
Introd.	. .	Introduction.
Ital.	. .	Italic letter.
Lev.	. .	Levant morocco.
Lge.	. .	Large.

Ll.	. .	Leaves.
L.P.	. .	Large paper.
L.s.	. .	Letter (not autograph), signed (p. 33).
Mco., mor.	.	Morocco.
M.e.	. .	Marbled edges.
MS(S).	. .	Manuscript(s).
N.d.	. .	No date.
N.p.	. .	No place, publisher, printer.
Ob., obl.	.	Oblong.
Oct.	. .	Octavo.
OED	. .	Oxford English Dictionary.
O.p.	. .	Out of print.
Or., orig.	.	Original.
P., pp.	. .	Page(s).
Pict.	. .	Pictorial.
Pl(s).	. .	Plate(s).
Pol.	. .	Polished.
Port.	. .	Portrait.
P.P.	. .	Privately printed.
Prelims. .	.	Preliminary leaves.
Pres.	. .	Presentation.
Pseud.	. .	Pseudonym(ous).
Pt.	. .	Part.
Ptd.	. .	Printed.
Pub(d). .	.	Publish(ed).
Qto.	. .	Quarto.
R.e.	. .	Red edges (p. 81).
Rev.	. .	Revised.
Rom.	. .	Roman letter.
S.a.	. .	*Sine anno*, undated (p. 139).
Sgd.	. .	Signed.
Sig.	. .	Signature.
S.l.	. .	*Sine loco*, no place of publication (p. 139).
Sm.	. .	Small.
S.n.	. .	*Sine nomine*, without name of printer or publisher (p. 139).
SOED	. .	Shorter Oxford English Dictionary.
Spr.	. .	Sprinkled.
Sq.	. .	Square (in shape).

STC	. .	Short-Title Catalogue.
Swd.	. .	Sewed.
T.e.g.	. .	Top edges gilt.
Thk.	. .	Thick.
T.L.s.	. .	Typed letter, signed (p. 33).
TLS	. .	Times Literary Supplement.
T.p.	. .	Title-page.
TS.	. .	Typescript.
Unb., unbd.	.	Unbound.
V.d., v.y.	.	Various dates, years.
V.g.	. .	Very good (copy).
Vol(s).	. .	Volume(s).
W.a.f.	. .	With all faults.
Wraps.	. .	Wrappers.
Y.e.	. .	Yellow edges (p. 81).

Abbreviations for SIZES OF BOOKS (see FORMAT)

Fo., Fol., 2°	.	Folio.
Qto., 4to, 4°	.	Quarto.
Oct., 8vo, 8°	.	Octavo.
12mo, 12°	.	Duodecimo (twelvemo).
16mo, 16°	.	Sextodecimo (sixteenmo).
24mo, 24°	.	Twentyfourmo.
32mo, 32°	.	Thirtytwomo.
64mo, 64°	.	Sixtyfourmo.

ADVANCE COPY

Within the past fifty years publishers have extended the practice of circulating advance copies of a new book to reviewers, chosen booksellers, judges of book-clubs, etc., besides those provided to their own travellers who will be 'subscribing' it to the trade. Such copies are normally either final PROOFS or the first to be gathered of the main run. They are often put up in plain or printed wrappers. But they may be bound; and if so the binding may occasionally retain a feature discarded in the published edition, or lack some final detail, or even be of a different colour or material (see TRIAL BINDING).

Such advance copies as show variations from the published edition, whether of text or binding, are naturally of interest to the keen collector. Even where no variations have yet been noticed, they are by their nature examples of an early state of the printed text (see ISSUES AND STATES), and they may on occasion be useful to the bibliographer confronted with a doubtful point in the published edition. But they do *not* (as is sometimes suggested) represent a first or early *issue* in the proper sense of the word; nor can the existence of fifty advance copies of a book prejudice in any way the firstness of the first edition as issued on the day of publication.

ADVERTISEMENTS

These have engendered as much heat and argument as any factor in book-collecting. It is first necessary to distinguish between:

(*a*) Leaves of advertisement, usually, though not necessarily, the publisher's, which are integral to the GATHERING (or quire or section), i.e. printed in the same operation with, and on the same paper as, and gathered for binding with, the sheets of the book itself;

(*b*) Leaves of advertisement—publisher's, wholesaler's, distributor's, or other—printed separately from the book and often on different paper, seldom peculiar to it, but bound up with all, or some, recorded copies.

The former date from the 16th century and were common in English books of the 17th and 18th. Their absence (discarded in binding or torn out later) incommodes the reader no more than the absence of a BLANK LEAF or a HALF-TITLE; for the text is not affected. But they may be bibliographically significant, and since, even if they are not, they are an integral part of the book, as intended by its publisher and executed by its printer, a copy cannot be considered as technically complete without them.

Inserted leaves of advertisements, usually in the form of publishers' lists or catalogues, are uncommon before the end of the 18th century, common in the 19th and early 20th centuries, and considerably less common since 1915.

Being wholesale appendages, they belong to the age of wholesale binding, whether in boards, wrappers or cloth. The normal practice would be for a publisher (or before the 1840s the wholesale distributor, who might not be the publisher) to provide his binder with a supply of some current list, with instructions to insert it either in specified books or in all his books as they came forward for binding. If the binder had no supply when he was ready to start, he would probably go ahead without; if the supply ran out, he would not wait for more, but would simply continue without the catalogue; or if he had a pile of an earlier list from the same publisher, he might use these up without regard to their being out of date. The hazards and permutations were as numerous as their results are often unaccountable.

Moreover, others besides the publisher whose name is on the title-page may in certain cases have been responsible for the wholesale binding, whether in boards, half cloth or (less often) cloth, of a part of the edition. A wholesaler for the provincial trade, an exporter to the colonial market, an Edinburgh or Dublin agent, a jobbing publisher who had bought a 'remainder' of the edition—any of these might buy in QUIRES, order his own binding, and insert his own catalogue (see WHOLESALER'S BINDING, REMAINDER BINDING). And if anyone wants to see how often such alien catalogues are found in PRIMARY bindings, especially of the boards period, he need only look through Michael Sadleir's *XIX Century Fiction*, where he will find dozens of examples.

As it has been a common practice since the early 19th century for such publishers' catalogues to be dated, their evidence in assessing priority between two observed variants of a book is sometimes useful. (It is obvious, for example, that copies of Trollope *The Warden* 1855 with an 1858 catalogue cannot have been among the earliest issued.) But it is evidence which must be used with great caution; and the classification of one copy of a book as a *first issue* because, though otherwise identical, its inserted catalogue is dated a month earlier than that found in another, is no more valid, without strong support from other arguments, than the proposition that a third copy is incomplete without any advertisements at all. An excellent example of a misleading sequence of advertisements is Wells *Tono Bungay* 1909, which is neatly dissected in Muir's *Points*, pp. 23, 24. And if the collector insists on having the publisher's catalogue in his copy of Maugham *Of Human Bondage* 1915, despite its absence from many demonstrably early-issued copies, he should remember that the same catalogue was used in half a dozen other Heinemann books published in the same season but less esteemed today, and look carefully to see whether a copy of one of these has not been deflowered to make him happy.

Books issued in PARTS present a special problem. For, casual as EDITION-BINDERS will often have been about inserting catalogues in cloth books, the assembly line for a popular mid-19th century part-issue must have been a nightmare, which experience suggests was only made sufferable to its operatives by an attitude so easy-going as to have amounted sometimes to levity. Cataloguers and bibliographers (see, for instance, Hatton & Cleaver's *Bibliography of Dickens's Novels issued in Parts*) have scrupulously noted every conformity to, or departure from, the complement of variegated slips, sheets, insets and the like, which has been accepted as the norm for any individual part in, say, *Ask Mamma* or *David Copperfield*. But how is the norm to be arrived at? The specialists have not always realised that the rarer the slip the less reason to suppose it a genuinely requisite component —and parts are MADE-UP more freely, and with wider approval, than any other class of book. A part-issue publisher would often farm out the contract for x thousand insertions, probably through an agent, to advertisers of mackintoshes and hair lotions; and the liability to confusion, casualness, shortages and mishaps in delivery from a dozen jobbing printers to the bindery multiplies a hundredfold the difficulty of establishing with confidence, a century later, the basic constituents. Which slips were, and which were not, included in the earliest, or even the large majority of the copies of some particular part, and with what degree of whose authority?

Part-issue collecting has its own special fascination, and its own rules (more of them made by enthusiasts than by rationalists). The general collector who wants a book in parts can either enter into the spirit of the thing and insist on a set with the sprig of heather or the bicycle clip in Part 19; or he can accept the more relaxed attitude which has gained a good deal of ground in the last thirty years—that provided you have correct text, plates and wrappers, plus perhaps any *publisher's* catalogue which ran steadily throughout the issue, the miscellaneous extras are optional rather than essential. They certainly had nothing to do with the author and, unlike the advertisements in cloth-bound books, they had very little to do even with the publisher, except as a source of revenue. It has to be admitted, however, that many of them are uncommonly entertaining.

ALL PUBLISHED

This means that, despite appearances or an original intention to the contrary, the volume or series described was not continued.

AMERICAN BOOK-PRICES CURRENT

Published annually since 1895 and for many recent years edited by Edward Lazare. Now divided into three sections: (1) printed books, etc., (2) autograph letters and manuscripts roughly divided chronologically into two series. The 1967 volume (published 1971) contained over 25,000 entries. Nothing is included which sold for less than ten dollars. Since 1958 ABPC, as it is commonly called, has included (without feeling the need, as yet, to change its title) the record of printed books (and, unlike its British competitor, of MSS) sold in the principal London auction houses as well as those of the United States.

AMERICANA

Books, etc., about, connected with or printed in America, usually, but not exclusively, the United States of North

America; or relating to individual Americans: as distinct (properly, though nowadays not invariably) from books by American writers. The *Columbus Letter* is a piece of Americana, as describing the discovery of the continent; the *Bay Psalm Book* as the first known book printed in what is now U.S.A.; and Thomas Paine's *Common Sense* as one of the influential documents of the War of Independence. Poe's *The Raven*, on the other hand, is not Americana, nor is Hemingway's *A Farewell to Arms*. Mark Twain's *Huckleberry Finn* or Thoreau's *A Week on the Concord and Merrimack Rivers* might be considered borderline cases, for if they are primarily outstanding works of American literature, they are also classically descriptive of the countryside and life of the people.

A currently fashionable sub-category should be mentioned: *Western Americana*. This embraces any piece of manuscript or printed matter documenting or deriving from the great westward expansion of the United States in the 19th century, from Lewis & Clark and the Louisiana and Gadsden Purchases down to Buffalo Bill and Frederic Remington.

Since Canada, Mexico, Central and South (or Latin) America are just as much part of the hemisphere as the United States, and since their ANA have keen collectors, there is beginning to be a need for a comprehensive word; for the narrower meaning of *Americana* is too firmly established (despite Mr. Wright Howes's regrettable attempt to introduce the uneuphonious term *USiana*) to be challenged.

ANA

A collective noun meaning a compilation of sayings, table talk, anecdotes, etc. Southey described Boswell's *Johnson* as 'the Ana of all Anas'. Its most familiar use is, however, the original one (from which the noun was made) in the form of a Latin suffix meaning material related to as distinct from material by; e.g. Boswelliana, Railroadiana, Etoniana. Like other such suffixes it is not always easily attachable to English names, even assisted, as commonly, by a medial *i*. Shaviana, Harveiana and Dickensiana are well enough; but Hardyana is repugnant to latinity; Cloughiana and Fieldingiana are awkward on the tongue; and should one write Wiseiana, Wiseana or Wisiana?

ANNUALS

Of books issued serially once a year two special classes have particularly interested collectors. (1) The anthologies of prose and/or verse, usually illustrated with steel engravings, which were a feature of late Regency and early Victorian publishing in England: copied originally from German and French models. Examples are *The Keepsake*, *The Book of Beauty*, *Friendship's Offering*, *The Literary Souvenir*. These were the gift books or 'table books' of the day, and many of them contain FIRST PRINTINGS of work by famous authors, often anonymous. (2) The Christmas annuals issued late in the 19th century by the publishers of popular or fashionable magazines; e.g. *Belgravia*, *The Mistletoe Bough*, *Tinsleys'*, *Routledge's*. These would often contain, and sometimes consist entirely of, a short novel by a contemporary best-seller or a promising dark horse.

ANONYMOUS

There is the formal anonymity of a book whose author, though his name is not on it, is known (e.g. *Gulliver's Travels*, *The Vicar of Wakefield* or *Sense and Sensibility*). For the cataloguing of these and similar pseudonymous books (e.g. *Alice in Wonderland* or *Jane Eyre*), some booksellers use, and others dispense with, the conventional square (or equally common round) brackets.

There is also, however, the real anonymity of 'authorship unknown'. And once in a while the cataloguer has to admit defeat. Since a book by an unidentified author is harder to sell (other things being equal) than one of known paternity, it may reasonably be assumed that he has consulted HALKETT AND LAING and the other obvious reference books. Yet *Anon* is an infrequent entry-heading in catalogues, less because there are not in fact many books whose authorship is unknown, than because anonymous titles are usually (and sensibly) listed under subject or category. There is generally a fair sprinkling among "Old Novels", and more amongst "Economics" or "Civil War Tracts".

ANTIQUARIAN BOOKSELLER

The lines of demarcation between 'rare books', 'old books' and 'second-hand books' have never been, and can never be, clearly defined. The same applies to most of those who deal in them; and the Antiquarian Booksellers' Association makes no distinction between a man who specialises in INCUNABULA, another who deals only in MODERN FIRSTS, a third who restricts himself to botany, and finally a general second-hand dealer, provided that his business is primarily in old books. The most comprehensive directories are those published by the Sheppard Press, London: *Dealers in Secondhand and Antiquarian Books in the British Isles* and *Book Dealers in North America* (arranged regionally as well as by specialities).

ANTIQUARIAN BOOKSELLERS' ASSOCIATION (INTERNATIONAL)

The British trade association, founded in 1906. Its badge may be seen on a good many booksellers' catalogues. A list of members can be had on application to the ABA's office, 9 Stanton Road, Wimbledon, London, S.W.20.

ANTIQUARIAN BOOKSELLERS' ASSOCIATION OF AMERICA

The trade association of antiquarian booksellers of the United States, founded in 1949. A list of members can be had on application to ABAA's headquarters, Store 2, Concourse, 630 Fifth Avenue, New York City.

ANTIQUE

(1) This has one specialised and superficially misleading use: for bindings (mostly CALF or HALF CALF) which are in fact modern but have been executed in the style of some earlier period. Alternative descriptions for this tactful approximation to the book's original dress would be 'old-style calf', or 'half calf, period style'.

ANTIQUE (continued)

Calf antique is also sometimes used to denote DIVINITY (or 'Oxford') calf.

Genuinely antique binding, if not precisely datable, will be described as original, contemporary, early, or simply old.

(2) A kind of paper, with a rough, uncalendered finish.

AQUATINT

See COLOUR-PLATE BOOKS, ILLUSTRATION
PROCESSES

ARMORIAL

As an adjective, used of (1) a binding blocked with the coat of arms, usually in gilt, of its original or a subsequent owner, and (2) of BOOK-PLATES based on, or incorporating, the owner's arms. As a noun, used colloquially for an armorially decorated book.

ART

When used of paper this adjective means a glossy or 'coated' variety. When used of a covering material, e.g. *art vellum*, *art leather*, it is a commercial abbreviation for artificial.

AS ISSUED

A term used to emphasise the ORIGINAL CONDITION, as issued, of the book described, especially when some individual feature contradicts normal expectation; e.g. 'edges trimmed, as issued', 'stitched, without wrappers, as issued', 'half roan, as issued'.

AS USUAL

A favourite qualification, among booksellers' cataloguers, to the admission of some defect or imperfection which is, or can be maintained to be, so prevalent as to be almost normal among copies of the book described: e.g. 'FOXED as usual', 'lacks HALF-TITLE as usual', 'Q4 is a CANCEL as usual', 'spine faded as usual'.

ASSOCIATION COPY

This term, often scoffed at by laymen, is applied to a copy which once belonged to, or was annotated by, the author; which once belonged to someone connected with the author or someone of interest in his own right; or again, and perhaps most interestingly, belonged to someone peculiarly associated with its contents.

The catalogue note will generally explain the nature of the 'association', which may vary from the obvious to the remote. An example of the former is Herman Melville's copy of *The Narrative of the Most Extraordinary and Distressing Shipwreck of the Whaleship Essex of Nantucket* (New York, 1821), with 18 pages of notes in his hand. A subtler one would be the copy of Maugham *Cakes and Ale* 1930 from the library of Hugh Walpole, who has generally been identified with one of the characters in the book. But only a cataloguer who despaired of selling a first edition of Norman Gale or F. W. Bain on its merits would dress it up as an 'association copy' on the grounds that it had (say) John Drinkwater's signature on the flyleaf.

If an entire section of a bookseller's catalogue is devoted to 'association books', it will often include PRESENTATION and INSCRIBED copies; but this is a loose application of a term which has its own proper and useful connotation.

A thoroughly bogus use of *association copy*, and one which should be actively resisted by collectors, is its application to a book of no importance in which there has been inserted (by an unknown hand) a letter by a person of some importance. A recent manual for book-collectors, for instance, described as 'an important item of Wildiana' a volume of old sermons in which someone had pasted, without visible connexion, a letter in Oscar Wilde's hand. This is stretching the meaning of 'association' well beyond the breaking-point.

AUCTIONS

This entry may conveniently be divided into four sections. (1) Catalogues. (2) Bidding. (3) Prices. (4) Terminology.

(1) The description of books, MSS., fine bindings, etc., in sale *catalogues* varies widely in fullness, precision and authority. The dressiest catalogues, unquestionably, are those of the Continental houses, with Paris perhaps the most lavish. Of late years, however, Sotheby's, the oldest and largest book-auction house in London, have tended to elaborate, especially for sales of importance or specialised interest, their conscientiously precise, but previously rather tight-lipped, descriptive formula; whereas the Parke-Bernet Galleries of New York, since 1964 affiliated with Sotheby's, are noticeably less promotional in style than in earlier days. Sotheby's Chancery Lane branch, long familiar as Hodgson's, specialises in books and cognate material, whereas Christie's book sales are a minor department of the firm's business. The catalogues of the provincial auctioneers, who are normally selling books as part of a mixed property, are often notably uninformative, especially as to the contents of bundled lots; and although legal warranty for the accuracy of descriptions of the lots offered is carefully restricted throughout the auction business as a whole, it is naturally a livelier issue in sales for which the catalogue makes no pretence to expertness. Yet the collector who contemplates bidding at an auction without professional advice would do well first to ponder the conditions of sale printed in every auction catalogue, which vary from firm to firm, and sometimes from sale to sale by the same firm; and then to remember that the return of any lot not actually incomplete or seriously mis-described will be (except with Charles Hamilton of New York, who blithely guarantees everything) a matter of grace, not of right.

The better auction houses, of course, take care to describe their offerings accurately, since 'returns' are just as much of a nuisance to them as to the buyer. (See, however, the separate entry NOT SUBJECT TO RETURN.) Despite occasional lapses, their cataloguers do their best to keep abreast of bibliographical research. And the annotation of important lots is often of a thoroughly scholarly character. In the description of fine early bindings, for example,

Sotheby's catalogues, thanks to the experienced connoisseurship of the Hobsons, *père et fils*, have achieved an authority shared by very few booksellers; and the same might of late years be said of the firm's cataloguing of manuscript material. Indeed, catalogues of famous libraries sold at auction have taken their place as indispensable reference books on the shelves, not only of booksellers and collectors, but also of scholars and librarians.

(2) Yet *bidding* at auction—any auction—is subject to many hazards besides the one well known in old wives' tales: that of the innocent bystander who nods her head without thinking and has a white elephant knocked down to her. This risk, if no other, can be avoided by entrusting one's bid to the auctioneer, who will execute it without commission, but also, of course, without assuming any additional warranty or exercising any such special discretion as is implicit in the employment of an agent.

There is the psychological risk: that one may be carried away by competitive fever. There is the economic fallacy: that any book bought at auction must be a bargain—a fallacy based on the supposition that all prices at auction sales are as it were wholesale, and that by buying in the rooms one cuts out the middleman (i.e. the bookseller). There is the risk of failure to realise that, while a bookseller guarantees his offerings, the rule in the auction room is *caveat emptor*. For once the hammer has fallen, the lot is yours; and if you find, when you get your books home, that one has been RE-CASED, another is not the first ISSUE, while a third is not as fine a copy as you had imagined, you will remember too late that the onus of satisfying yourself on these points has throughout been understood to be yours and not the auctioneer's.

Veteran collectors can, and sometimes do, bid for themselves without burning their fingers. They have examined their lots with care, they know what each book is worth (and also what they may have to pay, which is often not at all the same thing), and they are ready to pit their knowledge and sale-room tactics against those of the booksellers. Perhaps they simply enjoy an exhilarating session in the rooms. But they are still in a small minority; for most

experienced collectors have concluded that they are more
likely to get the lots they want, and get them at reasonable
prices, if they entrust their bids to a chosen bookseller.
Many collectors and institutional librarians employ a
regular agent for their auction business in each city. If not,
in selecting their man for a particular sale or a particular lot
they will probably have regard not only to his knowledge
and judgment, but also (especially in the more specialised
fields) to the advantage of eliminating a likely competitor
by making him their agent.

The normal commission charged by booksellers for
executing bids at auction is ten per cent, which may seem
expensive for a well-known and bibliographically un-
complicated book of high but stable market value—one,
that is, which does not involve much expert examination
or much expert estimation of price. But over a series of
transactions 'on commission' the bookseller will probably
engage a great deal more professional skill and spend a
great deal more time in his customer's interest than is
adequately repaid by his ten per cent. This of course is
payable only on successful bids; yet for the lots on which
he is outbid he will have provided equally full service—in
advice as to the probable price, in COLLATION and appraisal
of the material, in attendance (often with wearisome
waiting between lots) at the sale and in the highly skilled
business of the actual bidding.

The novice collector does well to recognise that in a
bookshop there is a strong bond of common interest
across the counter, but that in the sale-room every man's
hand (except the auctioneer's) is against him. If he is a
man of spirit, he may relish the encounter; hoping to beat
the professionals at their own game and prepared to take a
few knocks in the process. Yet if he is also a man of sense,
he will only do so after careful reconnaissance, and then
with his eyes wide open.

(3) *Prices* in the auction room, as listed in the annual
records, can be misleading unless they are carefully interpreted. For a reasonably common book—one, that is, of
which a copy or two turns up at auction every year—the

records provide a general idea of the level or trend of prices; and when, as often, these seem to fluctuate wildly, it must be remembered that one copy may have been in brilliant condition and the next one a cripple—a crucial difference which the abbreviated style of these records cannot be expected to make clear. For rarer books the occasional entries will, of course, provide some idea of the ruling price; but the more infrequent they are, the greater the need to consider the usually invisible factors—CONDITION (as always); but also, was this an important sale, when prices tend to be high? Or did the copy come up at the fag end of a miscellaneous one, when even booksellers tend to be weary and uninterested? Were there perhaps two keen collectors after the same lot, and therefore two exceptionally high commissions given? Or was this, by contrast, the purchase of a prudent bookseller buying for stock? Was there some POINT about the book, unmentioned in the sale catalogue (the source of the entry), which would account by its presence for a high price or by its absence for a low one?

It is also, of course, necessary to take into account the economic climate at the date when the price was reached. Many a book which brought a booming price in the Roxburghe sale in 1812, during the inflation of the Napoleonic wars, fell off in the twenties; and Heber's sale in the mid-thirties reflected an even severer depression. To take some more recent examples, prices were very high in certain categories (e.g. 18th century literature, the Romantics, modern first editions) during the 1920's. Prices across the board were low during the early and middle 1930's. Prices in many departments have risen steadily, in some sharply (e.g. science and medicine, colour-plate bird and flower books, modern literary manuscripts and correspondence) during the past twenty years. Moreover, an American considering a price record in sterling does well to remember that the sterling–dollar rate has fluctuated from time to time.

In short, the auction records have to be used with caution even for their main purpose, which is to give prices. As for the bibliographical information provided, at least by

the English annual, it should be treated with even greater
caution; for it is abbreviated (not always intelligibly)
from notes in the auctioneers' catalogues, which are themselves drawn from all sorts of sources—and have occasionally been known to include the happy excursions into
bibliographical theory and the optimistic estimates of
rarity which some collectors pencil on the flyleaves of their
favourite books. Even the most responsible auctioneers, it
will be recalled, are very careful to limit their assumption
of warranty; and their cataloguers, however expert, are
almost always working against time.

For a further qualification applicable to English sale-
room prices before 1927 (and even since) see RINGS.

For details of the annual records see AMERICAN BOOK-
PRICES CURRENT, BOOK AUCTION RECORDS and BOOK
PRICES CURRENT.

(4) In conclusion, a few miscellaneous notes. The
ownership of substantial or important properties sold at
auction is usually advertised. But the majority of sales in the
principal London and New York rooms are made up of
various properties, and a good many of these are apt to be
anonymous. This cloaking of ownership, which conceals
a book's immediate PROVENANCE, is sometimes due to the
modesty of the consignor (e.g. 'The Property of a Noble-
man Resident Abroad', 'The Property of a Lady'), or the
disinclination of a well-known collector to be identified
with the books he is discarding. More often it is simply
that the property is neither large enough nor important
enough (or the consignor newsworthy enough) to rate a
separate heading.

A proportion of these anonymous properties, however,
may come from some bookseller's stock: either because he
has bought a library containing a mass of books outside his
field; or because he has had certain books in stock for a
long time and is tired of offering them unsuccessfully; or
because he judges that some particular book will fetch a
better price at auction than he could get for it in his shop.
He may wish to reach a wider public than his own catalogue list; or he may have his eye on a collector who pre-

fers buying at auction to buying from a bookseller.

Then it must be realised that the vendor may have put a *reserve* on a lot, below which he is unwilling that it should be sold. The reserve figure has to be agreed with the auctioneer, who will treat it, in the strictest confidence, like any other bid committed to him by a would-be buyer and will bid from the rostrum. (It is illegal in England to put a reserve on a lot and then bid it up oneself or employ an agent to do so.) Lots which fail to reach the reserve and are knocked down to the owner (always under some assumed name) are said to be *bought in*; and the owner-purchaser will pay the auctioneer's commission, usually on a reduced scale. The last unsuccessful bidder on a lot at auction is known as the *under-bidder* or the *runner-up*.

AUTHOR'S BINDING

Copies to be presented by the author to his friends or to public figures were, from the earliest times, occasionally bound to his order; normally in a superior manner, but by no means always recognisable as such. (PANELLED MOROCCO was a common style for this purpose in the 17th and 18th centuries and VELLUM, gilt, in the 16th.) In the absence, therefore, of an inscription or other evidence, the statement that a leather-bound book is in an author's binding will usually be made—and should always be received—with caution.

During the age of PUBLISHER'S CLOTH, an author might occasionally have a dozen or more copies put up in a special style, or a different colour, for presentation to his or her friends: Lewis Carroll, Ouida and Mrs. Henry Wood provide a number of examples. But since the authenticated instances of this are rare, it is usually safer to presume that such bindings were a publisher's variant for the gift market (see GIFT BINDING) until the author's connexion has been proved.

AUTHORISED EDITION

When the collector of first editions is called upon to explain or defend his pursuit, he often emphasises the importance (as well as the sentimental appeal) of the earliest authentic text. But when he sees 'first authorised edition' in a catalogue description, that argument is apt to yield to his preference for chronological priority. For he will infer that this authorised edition was preceded by an unauthorised one; and even though he may take this opportunity of acquiring the former, he will nevertheless probably continue to covet the latter as well (and even more violently).

A good many 16th, 17th and 18th century books were first printed without their authors' consent—Browne *Religio Medici* 1642, Prior *Poems* 1707 and La Rochefoucauld *Maximes* 1664 are well-known examples, and Woodfall's authorised edition of *The Letters of Junius* (1772) was preceded by dozens of unauthorised ones. Such editions were printed sometimes from correct, sometimes from garbled manuscripts, furnished by or purloined from the friends among whom they were circulating. In the 19th century, popular works serialised in magazines were specially liable to piracy, whether Thackeray appearing in New York, Emerson in London or Balzac in Brussels earlier than from their accredited publishers.

To the French legitimacy is sacred and insularity traditional: *édition originale*, when used of a native author, means not first edition but the first authorised edition printed in France. In England and America, collectors and the trade have usually regarded a first unauthorised edition of domestic production as something to be taken seriously and priced much higher than the subsequent first authorised edition. The products of foreign enterprise are for the most part left to the keen author-collector.

See also 'FOLLOW THE FLAG', PIRACY.

AUTOGRAPH

In our world it is an adjective (and is better not used as a noun). It is applied to a manuscript, a letter or a document, either in the hand of, and preferably signed by, the author of one's choice, or on the subject of one's choice; or annotations in books, whether signed or not. The former are commonly described in abbreviated form, thus:

MS., MSS.   manuscript(s).
A.Ms.s.   autograph manuscript, signed.
A.L.   autograph letter, unsigned.
A.L.s.   autograph letter, signed.
L.s.   letter (in the hand of another), signed.
T.L.s.   typed letter, signed by hand.
A.D.s., or A.Doc.s., etc., means the same for *documents*.
A.N.s., etc. (rare), refers to a letter so short as to be no
more than a *note*.

See also HOLOGRAPH.

BACKED

(1) Of leaves, whether text or plates: see MOUNTED (2).
(2) Of the binding: this refers to a volume whose spine is
covered with a different material from the sides; e.g.
'marbled boards backed with leather', 'original boards
backed with cloth'. *Backed*, when used in this sense without qualification, almost always implies that the spine has
been re-covered at a later date with some alien material.
This is not quite the same thing as RE-BACKED, which
(again if unqualified) implies that the new spine is of the
same material—and sometimes in approximately the same
style—as the one it is replacing.

BACKSTRIP

A frequent synonym in the antiquarian book-trade for what
English publishers and edition-binders normally call the
SPINE or back of a book, and Americans the backbone or
shelfback: whether leather-bound, cloth-bound, boarded
or wrappered. *Back* is used in such terms as 'gilt back'
(of leather-bound books) or 'boards, cloth back' (see HALF
CLOTH), but should be, and mostly is, avoided in any
context where it might be confused with the back cover,
or lower board, of the binding.

BASIL

Heavily glazed sheepskin, usually of a dull crimson colour,
nowadays used mostly for ledgers and the like.

BASTARD TITLE

See HALF-TITLE

BEVELLED EDGES or BEVELLED BOARDS

A technique of binding in which the edges of the boards—usually extra thick boards—have been bevelled, i.e. cut to an oblique or slanting angle, before being covered.

BIBLIOGRAPHY

The word has two main meanings, really quite different, despite the fact that they may shade into each other in some cases. One (the more familiar to the general public) is a reading list, a guide for further study or a list of works which have been consulted by the author; and this will not normally give any detailed description of the books listed. The other, familiar to collectors, is the study of books as physical objects.

A bibliographer is a practitioner of the science in this latter sense. He may be also a librarian or a collector or a bookseller, an expert on an author or on the literature of a particular subject. But he need be none of these; nor are any of them *ipso facto* bibliographers. And bibliography, in this same sense, is the systematic description of books according to subject, class, period, author, country or district; or of the products of a particular press or publishing house. Bibliography may be enumerative, analytical or descriptive: ranging in scope and method (see DEGRESSIVE) from a HAND-LIST to a heavily annotated catalogue.

The kind which accounts for eighty per cent of the references in booksellers' catalogues is the *author-bibliography*: an account, whether in skeleton form or elaborate, of the printed works of a single author. This will normally be cited simply by the name of the bibliographer; so that the reader who finds attached to the description of a book by Donne the bare reference 'Keynes 27', to one by Gibbon, 'Norton 12' or to one by Galsworthy, 'Marrot, p. 63', may safely assume that these are the compilers of the standard bibliographies of those authors. He has, further, the right to assume that, unless anything is said to the contrary, the copy in question conforms exactly, in COLLATION and all other material details (the binding excepted, if earlier than *c.* 1830), to the description given in the bibliography cited.

Not all author-bibliographies, however, are of equal merit, and many are out of date. There are, also, books over which very respectable authorities disagree, where the unscrupulous cataloguer might be tempted to cite only the one who supports the copy he is describing. The judicious collector soon learns that verdicts are not infallible just because they are in print; that behind 'Latour's first issue' lurks the possible implication that Léoville is of a different opinion; that the cry of 'Not in Lafite' should excite him only if Lafite's book both claims to be comprehensive and has some reputation for accuracy; but that as long as others continue to cherish a VARIANT or an ISSUE canonised by however incompetent a bibliographer, so long will book-sellers continue to cite even an incompetent bibliography (if it suits them) rather than none at all.

BIBLIOMANIA
Literally, a madness for books. A *bibliomaniac* is a book-collector with a slightly wild look in his eye.

BIBLIOPHILY
The love of books. A lover of books is a *bibliophile*.

BINDER'S CLOTH
Any cloth binding, whether old or new, which is individual to the copy, i.e. not EDITION-BINDING. It is often used for collections of pamphlets, French novels or other paper-covered books which the owner did not think worthy of the dignity of leather. And from the collector's point of view it falls (with something of a thud) between two stools, for the contents are neither in ORIGINAL STATE nor hand-somely bound.

Binder's cloth is usually easy to distinguish, on stylistic grounds, from PUBLISHER'S CLOTH; for it is almost always lettered from type or from standard (not specially cut) dies, and if it is ornamented at all, the decoration is apt to be of conventional or even desultory character. The few exceptions date from the very early years of edition-binding in cloth (i.e. before about 1830), when both materials and style were still primitive; though REMAINDER bindings or LIBRARY bindings of later date are occasionally so degraded in style that the first example one sees might almost be taken for binder's cloth.

BINDER'S TICKETS

These are of two kinds. (1) During the last three quarters of the 18th century and the first quarter of the 19th, some binders signed their work with a small engraved or printed label, affixed usually to the top outside corner of one of the front ENDPAPERS. Thus, while a catalogue note which simply says 'by Derome le jeune' or 'by Staggemeier', or 'by Charles Hering', means that the cataloguer is reasonably confident that the book was bound by one of these masters, if he can add 'with his ticket' he has firm evidence for the attribution (and the price goes up accordingly). During the last hundred and fifty years or so these tickets have been for the most part superseded by the binder's name stamped (in gilt, in ink, or BLIND) on one of the inside boards, usually along the upper or lower edge. From the collector's point of view the modern method of signature has this advantage over the ticket that it cannot have been transferred, by some unscrupulous earlier owner or bookseller, from another book of less intrinsic interest.

See also SIGNED BINDINGS, PALLET.

(2) The other kind of ticket, very similar but usually printed, was used by some of the more substantial EDITION BINDERS—e.g. Westley, Burn, Edmonds and Remnant—during the middle and later decades of the 19th century, and was almost invariably placed at the inside lower corner of the back PASTE-DOWN endpaper. These tickets occasionally have some evidential value to bibliographers and, although seldom of importance to collectors, should always be recorded.

BINDING COPY

This means (or should mean) a copy whose covers are in a parlous state, but whose interior is clean and which is worth re-binding.

BINDINGS

This is a common subject-heading in booksellers' catalogues, and binding collectors have been heard to wish that
auctioneers would follow suit. Fine bindings have been
long and actively collected, and often therefore very highly
priced. But until the days of Weale and Gottlieb (say
1890–1910) research into binding history, and critical
attention to individual craftsmen and their patrons, lagged
so far behind enthusiasm that no statements made by
anyone else before 1920 should be taken for granted.

The past 40 or 50 years, however, have witnessed an
efflorescence of historical and critical scholarship in this
department; and if its published (or privately printed)
results are too expensive for the average collector to stock
his own reference shelves fully, he need only consult the
catalogue of the nearest well-found library under the names
of Strickland Gibson, E. Ph. Goldschmidt, G. D. Hobson,
J. B. Oldham, Ernst Kyriss, L. M. Michon, Charles Rams-
den, H. M. Nixon and A. R. A. Hobson to find that the
practitioners of the bibliopegic art in Europe, down to the
early 19th century at any rate, are by now beginning to be
properly documented.

He will not overlook the contributions of Seymour de
Ricci or Gordon Duff, nor the catalogues of such collectors
as Madame Whitney Hoff, J. W. Hely Hutchinson and
Major J. R. Abbey, nor those of such special exhibitions as
that held in the Baltimore Museum of Art in 1957/8 and at
the Pierpont Morgan Library in 1971. If he is curious, as he
should be, about functional as well as decorative develop-
ments he will consult Graham Pollard's paper on 'Changes
in the Style of Bookbinding, 1550–1830' (*The Library*,
June, 1956), which has been freely pillaged in the present
manual; and Bernard C. Middleton's *A History of English
Craft-Bookbinding Technique* 1963. If his interest embraces
publishers' bindings he will take as his springboard Michael
Sadleir's pioneer work, *The Evolution of Publishers'
Binding Styles* (1930).

See also SIGNED BINDINGS, ANTIQUE, ARMORIAL,
AUTHOR'S BINDING, CAMBRIDGE STYLE, CATHEDRAL
BINDINGS, COTTAGE STYLE, DIVINITY CALF, DOS-À-DOS

BINDINGS (continued)

BINDINGS, EDWARDS OF HALIFAX, EMBROIDERED BIND-
INGS, ETRUSCAN STYLE, FANFARE BINDINGS, GIFT
BINDING, GUTTA-PERCHA BINDING, HARLEIAN STYLE,
JANSENIST STYLE, LAW CALF, LIBRARY BINDINGS,
LYONNAISE, MOSAIC BINDINGS, MOTTLED CALF, ROMAN-
TIQUE STYLE, ROXBURGHE, ROYAL BINDINGS, SPANISH
CALF, TRADE BINDING, TREE CALF, TRIAL BINDING,
WHOLESALER'S BINDING.

BINDING MATERIALS

See BASIL, BINDER'S CLOTH, BOARDS, CALF,
CANVAS, CLOTH, CLOTH GRAINS and FABRICS,
CRUSHED MOROCCO, FOREL, HARD-GRAIN MOR-
OCCO, LEVANT, MOROCCO, NIGER, OASIS, PAPER
BOARDS, PARCHMENT, PIGSKIN, ROAN, ROUGH or
REVERSED CALF, RUSSIA, SCORED CALF, SHEEP, SKIVER,
STRAIGHT-GRAIN MOROCCO, TURKEY MOROCCO, VEL-
LUM, WRAPPERS.

BINDING TERMINOLOGY

See BACKED, BEVELLED, BLIND, BLOCKING, BORDER,
BOSS, CASED, CUIR-CISELÉ, DENTELLE, DIAPER, DICED,
DISBOUND, DOUBLURE, DRAWER-HANDLE, EXTRA,
FILLET, FRAME, FRENCH SEWN, FULL, GAUFFRED EDGES,
HALF BOUND, HALF CLOTH, HEAD-BAND, HOLLOW
BACKS, INLAID, INTERLEAVED, LABEL, LETTERING-
PIECE, LIMP, LININGS, MARBLED, MISBOUND, MITRE,
ONLAID, PALLET, PANEL, PASTE-DOWN, POINTILLÉ,
PRIMARY BINDING, PUBLISHER'S CLOTH, QUARTER
BOUND, RAISED BANDS, RE-BACKED, RE-CASED, RE-
JOINTED, REMBOÎTAGE, RE-SET, ROLL, SECONDARY
BINDING, SEMÉ, SPRINKLED, SQUARE, STAMPED,
STAPLED, STILTED, THREE-QUARTER BOUND, TOOLING,
TOP EDGES GILT, UNLETTERED, YAPP.

BINDING VARIANTS

A general term for the variations, whether of colour, fabric,
lettering or decoration, between different copies of the
same edition of a book bound (CASED) in publisher's cloth.
They are usually the result of the publisher's practice of
binding up an edition not all in one operation but in

batches as required; sometimes of his selling copies whole-sale in QUIRES for binding to another's order. See PUB-LISHER'S CLOTH, PRIMARY, SECONDARY, REMAINDER, AUTHOR'S BINDING, GIFT BINDING, LIBRARY BINDINGS.

BLACK LETTER
See GOTHIC

BLANCK

Bibliography of American Literature, by Jacob Nathaniel Blanck, Yale University Press for the Bibliographical Society of America, 1955 and onwards (still in progress).

By now commonly abbreviated to *BAL*, this is the most fully detailed bibliography of American literature (as distinct from AMERICANA) yet attempted.

BLANK LEAVES, BLANKS

Where these are an integral part of the book as completed by the printer, the bibliographer will record, and the fastidious collector will insist on, their presence, though the collector may make allowances in the case of a very rare book. Mere readers will prefer to remember the note printed, in Greek and Latin, on the otherwise blank leaf A9 of the Aldine Isocrates of 1513, which, freely translated, reads: 'This leaf is an integral part of the book, but cut it out if it bothers your reading, for it is nothing'.

Blanks sometimes occur at the beginning of the book, occasionally at the end of a clearly marked division, often at the end of the last GATHERING. In 17th century or earlier books an initial blank may, though rarely, carry a SIGNATURE letter; and occasional examples of this persist in more modern books.

In a leather-bound book it is necessary to distinguish these *printer's blanks* (sometimes signalised by cataloguers as 'blank and genuine') from any extra leaves which the binder may have used in the front or back—conveniently called *binder's blanks*. If the COLLATION calls for a blank leaf and the collector is in doubt whether the one present in his copy is the printer's (and so essential) or the binder's (and so irrelevant, or at least no substitute), let him compare

the texture of the paper, the direction and width of the
CHAIN-LINES, or the WATERMARK, if any, with those of
the paper in the body of the book.

If this test fails, let him open the book as wide as he dare,
examine the extreme inner edge of the doubtful leaf, and
see whether it is CONJUGATE with a leaf of the text or not.
The printer's blank should be: the binder's blank cannot be.

The blanks (variable both in incidence and in number)
used by mid-19th century American edition-binders when
CASING books in PUBLISHER'S CLOTH present a special
problem not yet solved by the bibliographers.

A blank leaf is provided for the fastidious collector ☞

BLIND
(OF TOOLING OR BLOCKING OR STAMPS)

When decoration or lettering on a binding is said to be
blind or *in blind*, this means that a plain impression has been
made in the leather or cloth by the tool, die-stamp or roll,
without any addition of gold or colour. E.g. 'contemporary
blind-tooled calf'; 'SECONDARY binding, in blue cloth with
the decoration in blind'. Similarly, 'blind stamp on title-
page' signifies that an owner's name or the words *Review
Copy, Presentation Copy* or the like have been impressed by
a die into the paper.

Blind impression, a term used by INCUNABULISTS, refers
to the accidental impress of uninked type on a blank page,
or part of a page, which sometimes throws light on the
circumstances of the book's printing or on the identity of
its neighbour in the press.

BLOCK, BLOCKED, BLOCKING

(1) In binding terminology a *block* is a piece of metal,
without a handle, bearing an engraved design for decorating the covers of a book, and intended to be used in a
press. The process of applying these is known as *blocking*,
and the press used is a blocking or arming press. Funda-
mentally the production of the so-called 'PANEL-STAMPED'
binding of the early 16th century was the same as that of
the gift book of the mid-19th. Both were blocked.

(2) The wood-block used by a wood-engraver (see WOOD-CUT): occasionally met with in such contexts as 'with fine, clear impressions of the engravings (most copies show the blocks badly worn)', or 'the original blocks are preserved in the Victoria and Albert Museum'.

BLOCKBOOKS

Blockbooks, or xylographica, as produced in Europe—usually with more illustrations than text, often hand-coloured, and mostly of a popular and/or religious character—were long supposed to have preceded the invention of printing from movable metal types (by Johann Gutenberg, *c.* 1440–50). Recent research, however, much of it conducted by the late Allan Stevenson into their paper, has established that (despite the solitary example of the unique *Apocalypse I* in the Rylands Library, which he dated *c.* 1451) the heyday of the blockbook was in fact the 1460's, to which the early and famous examples—whether *Apocalypse, Biblia Pauperum, Ars Moriendi, Cantica Canticorum* or *Speculum Humani Salvationis*—have been proved to belong. Many others, mostly of lower price and quality, belong to the 1470's, while isolated specimens continued to appear up to *c.* 1500.

The blockbook was essentially a picture book, the illustration and its accompanying text being cut with the knife on wood and printed on one side of the paper only. They were often, perhaps normally, impressed from two-page blocks reaching across the sheet, in a brownish or greyish water-based ink (only from *c.* 1470 was oil-based ink generally used, thus allowing printing on both sides of the leaf). Examples are nowadays of extreme rarity, cost a great deal of money, and will be beyond the horizon of most collectors.

BLURB

A slang word, borrowed from the vocabulary of the publishing business, and irreverently applied to those puffs or 'write-ups' with which booksellers sometimes embroider their catalogues. The blurb is quite distinct from the note

of literary description or background which, for important
or obscure books, often follows the physical and bibliographical particulars. It is essentially persuasive or lauda-
tory. And it comes in a number of styles: (i) the quotation,
or second-hand advertisement; (ii) the original composition, impersonal; and (iii) the ostentatiously personal.

Type (i) usually takes the form of a sentence or two of
praise culled from an established critic—Johnson, Hazlitt,
Matthew Arnold, Saintsbury, Lytton Strachey—or, if that
has proved elusive, from the *Dictionary of National
Biography*, the *Cambridge History of English Literature* or
even the *Encyclopædia Britannica*. A variation is the
anecdotal; e.g. 'Macaulay is reputed to have read all four
volumes of this book at a sitting', or 'General Burgoyne
said he would rather have written this poem than capture
New York'.

Type (ii) is probably the commonest, and it varies
widely with the character (and prose style) of the cataloguer. But there are three main subdivisions: the solid
but dull—e.g. 'This is the chief work of the eminent
French essayist'; the enthusiastic—e.g. 'It is impossible
to overestimate the importance of this great speech in the
annals of American history'; and the picturesque—e.g.
'This book was, as it were, the first shot in the Marxist
revolution'.

Type (iii) is sometimes categorical—e.g. of an 1880's
reprint of the Waverley novels, 'Scott was one of George
Eliot's favourite authors—difficult to think of higher
praise than that for any writer'; and sometimes defiant—
e.g. 'Despite the indifference of contemporary critics, here
is an author who will be read when most of today's idols
are forgotten.'

Blurbs annoy some collectors, amuse others, possibly
influence a few. Good ones are much harder to write than
you think.

BOARDS

(1) In the widest sense, the wood, paste-board, strawboard or other base (not leather) for the sides of any bound

or CASED book, i.e. any book in hard covers. As commonly used, the term includes the covering of the actual board (usually paper), thus—'old marbled boards, calf back', 'blue-grey boards, canvas back, Kelmscott style', 'front board detached, but a clean copy', 'new boards, leather label'. Purists describe the covers of a book in PUBLISHER'S CLOTH as *cloth boards*.

(2) Also used in a specialised sense, to mean the *original* boards, backed with paper, in which many books were temporarily encased for distribution between about 1740 and 1780, and most books between 1780 and the 1830's, when EDITION-BINDING in cloth began to take hold. Thus—'the boards-and-label period', 'second issue in cloth, the first issue being in boards', 'nice copy in half calf of a book virtually unprocurable in boards', 'the Kern copy in boards was sold for $13,000'. But the collector who has become infatuated with the charm of original boards will do well never to assume that the term *boards*, in a *catalogue description* of a book, is necessarily being used in sense (2). When a bookseller is offering a book in *original* boards he will usually say so.

BOOK AUCTION RECORDS

Published annually (and for a period also in quarterly parts) since 1902.

For some observations on auction *prices* see under AUCTIONS (3) Prices. BAR covers the principal British and American sales, with a selection of others, listing items which fetched £5 or more, but excluding composite lots or bundles. It does not record manuscripts or autograph letters.

BOOK FORM

A term used to distinguish the first appearance of any work in a book from an earlier FIRST PRINTING in a periodical, series of proceedings, BROADSIDE, leaflet or the like. For instance, a Churchill speech might be first printed in *The Times*, then in Hansard, then possibly in a party leaflet; but unless it was issued as an individual unit between its

own covers, its 'first edition in book form' would probably be a collected volume of speeches, issued perhaps
several years later. Similarly, John McCrea's poem, 'In
Flanders fields the poppies blow', was published in *Punch*
in 1915; but its first edition in book form was an anthology
called *In the Day of Battle*, Toronto, 1916.

The term may also be applied to the author: e.g.
Catholic Anthology 1915 was T. S. Eliot's 'first appearance
in book form'.

Of a book first issued in PARTS, the more usual term is
'first edition in *volume* form'.

BOOK-LABEL

A label of ownership, usually affixed to one of the front
endpapers and (whether engraved or printed) simpler in
style and smaller than a book-plate. It will normally
consist merely of the owner's name.

BOOK-PLATE (or EX LIBRIS)

"The size of a book-plate", said William M. Ivins, "is
usually in inverse proportion to the owner's interest in
books." Book-plates may be of artistic interest ('fine Chip-
pendale book-plate in all four volumes') or they may help to
establish the book's PROVENANCE by identifying an earlier
owner. Even when they have no apparent interest, it is absurd
to regard them as a blemish ('book-plate on front endpaper,
otherwise a fine copy'), unless the art work is so ugly as to
qualify as a blemish in its own right. They are not, however,
too difficult to remove—and replace. Thus, the collector
who is attracted to a copy of some considerable book
because it has, say, Gibbon's or Horace Walpole's book-
plate should scrutinise it with care, for many inconsiderable
books from both libraries have been in circulation for a
good many years, and one of these may have yielded up its
book-plate.

BOOK PRICES CURRENT

A record of prices fetched at auction, published annually
from 1887 to the season 1947/8 and then twice at four-year
intervals. Now abeyant.

See note to BOOK AUCTION RECORDS. BPC's formula of description was somewhat fuller than BAR's: it covered approximately the same ground.

BOOK-STAMP (or LIBRARY STAMP)

An ownership stamp of metal or rubber applied in ink or BLIND to an endpaper or fly-leaf, or to the cover by an impressed metal die, whether gilt or blind.

BOOKSELLERS' CATALOGUES

These range, in pretension, from the mimeographed sheet headed *Secondhand Books* to the cloth and gold volume listing *Fifty Rare Books and Manuscripts*, with a full-page illustration of each. They are of many shapes, sizes and styles: general, semi-specialised, specialised; well or ill, enticingly or dispiritingly, thoughtfully or conventionally printed; personal or impersonal in content, and in annotation (see BLURB); detailed or sparing, reliable or unreliable, in description of the CONDITION of the books offered; conservative or dashing in bibliographical speculation (see ISSUE-MONGERS); scholarly, businesslike, or casual; sometimes carefully and consistently priced, sometimes erratically or even waywardly; arranged alphabetically, or by subject, or by date, or sometimes simply huggermugger ('I want the customer to read right through, not skip'); with the one common denominator that, to a true collector, they are all worth reading.

A general catalogue would need to contain many very fine or some especially interesting things for the average collector to give it permanent shelf-room. Most people, whether amateurs or professionals, tear out and file, rather than face the inexorable, un-indexed accumulation. Specialised, and even semi-specialised, catalogues are another matter; and whether one binds in groups or series, files in boxes, or shelves in some sort of order, a selection of the booksellers' catalogues of the past is one of the most important and most frequently consulted departments in any alert collector's reference library. This is not merely for the comparing of prices: it is for the contributions to scholarship, bibliographical and other, which responsible antiquarian booksellers have made, and make, every year.

The citation of examples is too invidious a task to be pursued as fully as my own obligation to the catalogues of the trade naturally inclines me, nor do I care even to seem to impugn, by omission, the well-thumbed favourites on every reader's shelf. Let two, then, suffice: the series *Bibliotheca Chemico-Mathematica* prepared for Henry Sotheran & Co. by Dr. Zeitlinger—a pioneer omnibus for collectors of scientific books; and the *Catalogue of Type-founders' Specimens* etc., prepared by Mr. Graham Pollard for Birrell & Garnett in 1928, which is one of the standard reference books in its field.

BORDER

When used in descriptions of binding, whether of leather or cloth, this properly means decoration that closely borders the edges of the cover (cf. FRAME).

BOSS

Metal knobs used by the early binders, originally to protect the surface of the leather sides, but often incorporated in the decoration.

BOUND

In a bound book, whatever the material which is to cover the sides and spine, the folded sections of printed matter are sewn on to horizontal cords (usually four or five), the free ends of which are then drawn through holes in the boards and firmly attached. The result is that leaves and binding become a structural entity before the covering material is glued or pasted on to the boards (cf. CASED).

BREAKING-UP

COLOUR-PLATE books are often broken up and the plates sold separately for framing. The text will be thrown away. Book-collectors regard this as vandalism; and reasonably, since it destroys a book. Print-sellers and people furnishing houses would no doubt plead the greatest happiness of the greatest number. Except for bulky encyclopædias and the like, most booksellers dislike breaking-up a complete book (incomplete copies are another matter); but this respect for an entity seldom survives a market development which makes separate plates easier to sell and more profitable.

BREAKING COPY, or BREAKER

A book, especially a COLOUR-PLATE book, which is so seriously imperfect that it seems fit only for BREAKING-UP. Besides picture books, rare early printed books in fragmentary state are sometimes thought suitable 'breakers' for typographical collections; and the practice is also applied to literary treasures—e.g. single plays extracted from an imperfect Shakespeare folio, or single books from a 1611 Bible. The term *breaker* is also sometimes applied to the man who habitually does so.

THE BRITISH MUSEUM CATALOGUE OF BOOKS PRINTED IN THE FIFTEENTH CENTURY
The first volume published in 1908 : still in progress.

Although this is only one of many special catalogues issued by the British Museum in addition to its general catalogue, it is the one most commonly cited by booksellers, usually by the abbreviation BMC. Arranged on PROCTOR'S principles, it is less convenient for first reference than HAIN or GOFF, which are alphabetical; and containing only the books in the Museum's collections, it is not so complete as the GESAMTKATALOG will be if it is ever finished. But (apart from being in English) its admirable introductions and plates, and its vast range, make it an indispensable reference book for even a desultory collector of INCUNABULA. A lithographic reprint of vols. I–IX (Germany, Italy, France, Holland and Belgium) contains corrections and notes from the departmental copies.

BROADSIDE or BROADSHEET

'A large sheet of paper printed on one side only' (SOED). Strictly, neither term should be applied to any but a whole, undivided sheet. Bibliographers abbreviate it to 1°.

BROCHURE

A genteel, and superfluous, synonym for a PAMPHLET.

BROKEN TYPE

Since the commonest cause of broken or damaged type is wear and tear in the course of printing, observed deterioration as between copies of the same edition may help (especially in 19th and 20th century books) to distinguish between IMPRESSIONS, ISSUES or STATES of that edition. It is, however, evidence which must be applied with caution, and the collector should beware of its frequent abuse by ISSUE-MONGERS. Probably more books than not have a broken letter somewhere, or a faultily printed letter which looks like one; just as there are few books without a misgrint. And no encouragement should be given to the excited cataloguers who rush to draw unwarrantable conclusions from either.

BRUNET

Manuel du Libraire et de l'Amateur de Livres, by Jacques-Charles Brunet, 5 vols., Paris, 1860–64, with a sixth volume of *Table,* and two supplementary vols., 1878–80. Also a recent reprint.

Despite its age, Brunet is still a valuable general reference book of international scope.

CALF

Leather made from the hide of a calf: the commonest leather used in bookbinding. It is smooth, with no perceptible grain. Its natural colour is pale biscuit but it can be dyed almost any shade.

Calf can be treated in a number of ways, and for books full bound (as distinct from HALF BOUND) it will often be further described as polished, SPRINKLED, MOTTLED, stained, TREE (a special pattern), MARBLED, DICED, SCORED or grained. There are also special styles, such as ROUGH, or reversed, DIVINITY, LAW and ANTIQUE.

In catalogues, *calf* (unqualified) will usually denote a binding not so new as to be shiny and not more than about a hundred years old; *old calf,* a binding clearly not modern, but one which the cataloguer does not consider contemporary with the book and hesitates to date with any precision; *early calf* (which would not be used of a book printed later than about 1750), one seemingly bound (or rebound) fairly soon after publication, but not close enough to it to justify the adjective *contemporary*.

For the considerations which govern (or ought to govern) the use of the term *original calf*, see TRADE BINDING, ORIGINAL STATE.

CALLED FOR

A favourite expression with booksellers' cataloguers; e.g. 'without the advertisement leaf called for by Hock', 'with the misprint on p. 113, as called for by Sherry', 'with the half-title in volume 2 (none called for in volume 1)'. The authority relied on will usually be mentioned by name; but in a fair number of cases, like the third above, we are expected to conform to some anonymous and thus more potent fiat. For while it is permissible to dissent from a named bibliographer, an undefined body of assumed knowledge is beyond the reach of argument.

CALLIGRAPHY

Calligraphy has been defined by Mr. Stanley Morison (in the *Encyclopædia Britannica*) as 'freehand in which the freedom is so nicely reconciled with order that the understanding eye is pleased to contemplate it'. In our context the noun and its adjective *calligraphic* are used not only to denote a manuscript whose beauty of SCRIPT is its principal attraction, or a manual of penmanship, or an engraved WRITING BOOK, but also any fancy penwork in a manuscript or inscription or any non-representational flourishes in an engraving.

THE CAMBRIDGE BIBLIOGRAPHY OF ENGLISH LITERATURE
Edited by F. W. Bateson, 4 vols., 1940, Supplement edited by George Watson, 1957. New edition in progress.

Although cited by booksellers less often than might be expected, CBEL is the only serious attempt since

LOWNDES to produce a bibliographical survey of the whole of English literature. It includes every writer who could be called an author, with SHORT-TITLE and first publication date of their works, important reprints, revised editions, critical and biographical works, etc., etc. Dates given for original editions are naturally not infallible.

The sections arranged under the more specialised headings contain some of the most valuable information in the book; and Mr. Graham Pollard's articles on book production and distribution, libraries, newspapers, etc., demand special mention in the present context.

CAMBRIDGE STYLE
(OF BINDING)

Bookbinders have used this term for at least a century to denote an originally Restoration style of CALF binding with PANELLED sides: a rectangular FRAME left plain with the central rectangle and border MOTTLED or SPRINKLED. Though doubtless used elsewhere, this style was such a favourite with the binders of Cambridge in the early years of the 18th century as to have been recognised as a speciality: hence presumably its name (sometimes in the form *Cambridge pane*).

CANCELS

'A cancel is any part of a book substituted for what was originally printed. It may be of any size, from a tiny scrap of paper bearing one or two letters, pasted on over those first printed, to several sheets replacing the original ones. The most common form of cancel is perhaps a single leaf inserted in place of the original leaf' (MCKERROW). The maximum number of substitute leaves which, collectively, still qualify for the term *cancel* (in the singular) has apparently never been laid down.

Cancels, being testimonies to human error, have been common since printing was invented, and they were particularly common in the 17th and 18th centuries. With the development of high-speed machinery during the past hundred years it has become progressively easier and cheaper to reprint the two- or four-leaf fold or even the whole GATHERING in which the fault has been found than to insert a separate substitute leaf. But this alternative is normally adopted only if the error is discovered before the quires are stitched; and there are therefore plenty of exceptions—Swinburne *Poems and Ballads* 1866 and Maugham *The Painted Veil* 1925, for instance, were peppered with single-leaf cancels.

The original sheet or leaf is called the cancelland (or *cancellandum*). That which is printed to replace it is called the cancel (or *cancellans*). A substitute fold will be sewn in, but a substitute leaf is stuck on to the STUB of its cancelland.

In default of external evidence it is usually impossible to tell whether the process of cancelling a leaf or leaves was carried out before or after the book was published. If before, the result will be two states of the book; if after, two issues. (See ISSUES AND STATES.) But in either case the earlier, uncorrected form of the passage will be of interest; and it may be of great interest if the correction was not merely a verbal or grammatical one, but represented a change of thought, an addition or (as often) a suppression by the author.

The usual method for indicating to the binder that a certain leaf was to be cancelled was to slit it upwards at the foot. Occasionally a leaf slit in this way, having been overlooked by the binder, will be found bound up in the book (with or without its substitute). It should not be mistaken for a leaf which has been carelessly or accidentally torn. The *cancellans* would often be given a SIGNATURE mark (sometimes asterisked), whether the *cancellandum* had one or not.

Cancel title-leaves. In seventeenth-century England a publication would often be shared between two or more bookseller-publishers, each of whom might have his own IMPRINT on his share of the edition. Although these copies were normally published simultaneously, all the variant title-leaves except one will probably be cancels. (Well-known examples are Herbert *The Temple* 1630 and Locke *Humane Understanding* 1690.)

A different type of cancel title (making an issue, not a state) results from the unsold copies of a book being furnished either with a later-dated title from the original publisher (e.g. Henry Vaughan *Silex Scintillans* 1650–55, Trollope *The MacDermots of Ballycloran* 1847–48) or that of another publisher who had taken over the book (e.g. *Paradise Lost* 1667–69, *Lyrical Ballads* 1798, the Brontës' *Poems* 1846).

The collector who wishes to pursue cancels beyond McKerrow is recommended to R. W. Chapman's monograph, *Cancels* (Bibliographia Series, No. 3, 1930).

CANVAS

A material used mostly for rough jobbing binder's work. Exceptions are (1) certain kinds of chapbooks and educational books, which were issued between about 1770 and about 1830 bound in plain buff canvas or canvas-buckram. (2) The spines of board bindings on PRIVATE PRESS, *de luxe*, or other slightly self-conscious books from William Morris's Kelmscott Press (1891) onwards. (3) Certain special classes of reference book; e.g. until recently the transactions and other publications of the Bibliographical Society.

CAPTION

When this word was first borrowed from legal phraseology and applied to books, it meant 'the heading of a chapter, section or article' (OED). But it is now generally used to mean the title or line of text under an illustration. Other names for this are *underline* and *legend*.

CARTOUCHE

A tablet, for inscription (e.g. the titling of maps) or ornament; originally in the form of a scroll, but sometimes used loosely (especially in descriptions of bindings) for round, oval or decorated labels.

CASED

(AS OPPOSED TO BOUND)

In a cased book the boards and their covering material are made up separately, in quantity. The stitched quires, held together by a strip of canvas (called *mull*) glued on to their backs, are inserted into the ready-made case by machinery. They are attached by gluing the overlaps of the mull—sometimes also tapes or threads—to the inner edges of the boards, over which the ENDPAPERS are then pasted down.

Casing has been the normal method of EDITION-BINDING for more than a hundred years; and although the result, which is a ready-to-wear not a tailored job, cannot compare with binding for durability, it is perfectly adequate for cloth-bound books. Today, indeed, casing is so much taken for granted that the words *bound* and *binding*—as in 'cloth-bound' or 'publisher's binding'—are used without regard to the important technical distinction between the two methods.

The casing method is also used for covering books in leather.

CASES AND BOXES

These are specially made to measure for the preservation of precious or fragile books. The four commonest kinds are: (1) the slip case, (2) the fall-down-back box (of which the SOLANDER CASE or box is an aristocratic version), (3) the pull-off case, and (4) for pamphlets and wrappered books of slender bulk, the four-fold wrapper or portfolio with flaps.

The *slip case* is generally open-faced to show the spine of the volume or volumes. If so, the open end may be leather-edged (a style popular in France). It should have either thumb-holes or a ribbon-pull, unless the book is to be shaken or poured out. If slip cases are too loose, the book falls out; if too tight, it is damaged at the edges every time it is taken out or replaced, unless this is prevented by wrapping the book in a two-fold or, more commonly, four-fold folder, before it is slipped into the case. This treatment, however, prevents any part of the book being visible on the shelf.

The *fall-down-back box* has a double-hinged spine, so that it lies flat when opened. The lower half holds the book to be preserved and the upper half closes upon the lower. It may be of full or half leather (more often MOROCCO than CALF), of cloth or buckram (either with a leather label or lettered direct), or even (rarely) of paper-covered boards. It is for most purposes, if well built and well fitted, the most satisfactory kind for books, for the volume or volumes can be taken out and put back with the minimum risk of damage, and it can be opened to display its contents without their necessarily having to be handled at all—an important point if a precious book is being shown to some possibly ham-fisted layman.

The *pull-off case* is almost always made of leather, is airtight (a dubious advantage) and sometimes has an asbestos lining (it is the only kind which can be fire-proofed). It is made in two halves, the book being placed in the lower and the upper then fitted on to it.

The question whether or not to enclose a book for its better preservation (incidentally cutting it off from the circulation of air) is often a difficult one; and practice varies more with the taste of individual collectors than with climatic or practical considerations. A row of cloth boxes does not make much of a show on a bookshelf, and even the most elegant LEVANT solanders or pull-offs, though many people think very highly of their appearance, some-how never look at all like books. Furthermore, to examine or display a book preserved in a pull-off case, or any case with an inner folder, requires three hands and a table-top. Yet without some sort of case, pamphlets can hardly stand comfortably on a loose shelf, nor be easily replaced on a tight one. Fragile volumes, whether in wrappers, boards, friable cloth or leather weak at the joints, are liable to damage and deterioration on the open shelf, and ought to be protected; as, no doubt, ought painted or elaborately decorated bindings. But to put a plainly and solidly bound book in a box is seldom necessary, and to do so (as is done) with one recently bound is surely mere ostentation. Yet even those who dislike cases will admit that they are sometimes necessary; and it may be recalled that the most obnoxious kinds—the slip-in case and the pull-off—have an ancestry which goes back at least as far as the 18th century.

Whatever general policy the collector decides to adopt, or whatever decisions he makes in individual instances, he will realise that booksellers are more prone to boxing and casing than he himself need be: for three special reasons. One is that a bookseller may have a book exposed to the public on his shelves for some time, so that a not too expensive case fulfils for him a function similar to that of the dust-jacket on a new book. It also helps to ensure respectful handling by potential purchasers. Secondly, he may think (often correctly) that any book in a box has a more impressive and expensive look than the same book without one. And thirdly, if he has a rather poor copy of a book, he may consider (again often correctly) that a handsome case will distract attention from a stained or shaky binding.

CATALOGUE NOTES
See BLURB

CATCHWORD

'The first word of the following page inserted at the right-hand lower corner of each page of a book, below the last line. (Now rarely used.)' Thus SOED. (*E.g. the word of at the foot of this page*.) The collector who is not a bibliographer is likely to have to concern himself with catchwords only in two contexts. First, they will sometimes be referred to where they are (or are thought to be) involved in some POINT—e.g. of Goldsmith *She Stoops to Conquer* 1773, 'the state with the catchword "Tony" on N2 verso'. Secondly, it is always wise, when considering a CROPPED copy of an early book, to make sure that no catchwords have been trimmed off or cut into.

CATHEDRAL BINDINGS

This term is applied to bindings decorated with Gothic architectural motifs—often including a rose window—produced in France and England between *c.* 1810 and *c.* 1840. In England this decoration was sometimes built up

57   of

of large single tools. In France the designs were normally BLOCKED on the covers.

CHAIN LINES

The widely spaced lines (distinct from the lighter, close-set lines which run at right angles to them) visible in the texture of LAID paper, made by the wire mesh at the bottom of the tray in which it is made. They are sometimes imitated in machine-made papers.

If there is any doubt about the genuineness or, in the case of BLANKS, relevance of a leaf or leaves in a book printed on laid paper, the chain lines, which vary in spacing between different papers, offer a useful preliminary check.

CHAPBOOKS

Small pamphlets of popular, sensational, juvenile, moral or educational character, originally distributed by chapmen or hawkers, not by booksellers. Not in current use since about 1830, except as a conscious archaism (e.g. Field and Tuer's publications in the 1890's, Lovat Fraser's *Flying Fame* series, etc.).

CHEAP COPY

When a collector sees a book described as 'a cheap copy', he will be well advised to study the list of defects which generally accompanies such a description. Purists and speculators seldom buy such copies. The former would rather wait for a fine one, even though it will cost more; the latter learns from experience that defective copies, however cheap, are rarely bargains in terms of resale. But for the modest collector who knows that a fine copy of some book he covets will always be beyond his means, a 'cheap copy', taken with his eyes open, may be an acceptable compromise between a fine one and none at all.

See also CONDITION.

CHECK-LIST

An increasingly popular term, of American origin (1853), which is sometimes used for, and could usefully be confined to, something less full than a HAND-LIST (1859), but fuller than a SHORT-TITLE or 'finding' list; but which in common usage is virtually synonymous with a hand-list.

CHINA PAPER

A very thin, soft, absorbent paper, made in China from bamboo fibre, yellowish or greyish or straw-coloured, used for PROOFS of ENGRAVINGS or WOODCUTS, and occasionally also for lithographs. The proofs are usually pasted on to stouter paper. Sometimes called *India Proof Paper*. There are European imitations.

THE CHRONOLOGICAL OBSESSION

The importance attached to chronological priority—first edition, first issue and so on—looms so large in modern book-collecting that a novelist describing a bibliophile, or the man-in-the-street apologising for an eccentric friend, will say that so-and-so 'collects first editions'. Many of the hoariest gibes against book-collecting are provoked by the same excusable misconception. Yet the predominance of this particular factor among the many which may make a book interesting, desirable or important is actually of quite recent development (the average 19th century collector was as much interested in the finest-looking or best-edited edition as in the first); and some good judges regard it as both parochial and probably transitory.

Nevertheless, many collectors and booksellers and bibliographers have allowed their zealous preoccupation with the minutiæ of priority to become an obsession. A glance at such entries as ADVANCE COPY, TRIAL ISSUE, MISPRINTS, ISSUE AND STATE, 'FOLLOW THE FLAG', or PRE-FIRST will show some of the forms which this obsession takes; and if a slightly acid note is discernible in the comments offered there and elsewhere in this book on the more extreme manifestations of priority-consciousness, it must be set down to the conviction that all extremes are a bore.

CLOTH

The commonest material used for the binding (strictly the CASING) of books as published in the English-speaking

CLOTH (continued)

countries since the second quarter of the 19th century. There is a sharp distinction between PUBLISHER'S CLOTH and BINDER'S CLOTH, and the unqualified description *cloth* in a bookseller's catalogue (unless devoted exclusively to quite modern books) does not necessarily imply the former.

See also COLOURS OF CLOTH, HALF CLOTH.

CLOTH GRAINS AND FABRICS

The classification and nomenclature of the basic fabrics used for PUBLISHER'S CLOTH binding are not yet standardised in bibliographical description. It is only, indeed, during the past half century that the problem has begun to receive any serious attention, and then only from a handful of bibliographers.

It was first systematically attacked by Michael Sadleir, in his *Evolution of Publishers' Binding Styles* (1930). His classification, based on historical principles, capable of family grouping, descriptive in nomenclature, was developed in my own *Binding Variants in English Publishing, 1820–1900* (1932). Sadleir further expanded and refined it in his catalogue of *XIX Century Fiction* (1951), with illustrations of a wider range of typical 19th century cloth grains than the earlier works provided. (Reprinted in *The Book Collector*, vol. 2, no. 1, 1953.)

Some recent bibliographers of authors of the period 1830–90 (since when differences of fabric are both less conspicuous and generally less often significant) have adopted the Sadleir system, albeit rather gingerly. Others have seemed to decline its niceties. The only alternative system so far produced keys a specific fabric by letter to the nowadays approximately standardised sample-books of the book-cloth manufacturers, with notional letters for patterns no longer (or never) therein designated. This system, though it is capable of greater precision in identification, was considered and rejected by Sadleir and myself in the early thirties, as being mechanical, inelastic and virtually impossible to memorise: but it has been adopted, with all the authority of the Bibliographical Society of America, in Mr. Jacob Blanck's *Bibliography of American Literature*

(Yale University Press, in progress), with explanation in vol. I and the key plate repeated in succeeding volumes. It would ill become me to express a preference between the two. Use will decide.

COLLATION

In the sentence, 'this copy has been collated with the one in the British Museum', the cataloguer is using the word in its simpler sense of 'to compare'; and the implication is that the two copies are of the same composition. When he pencils on the endpaper 'collated and perfect' (or simply 'c. & p.'), he is using it in the special sense of 'to examine the sheets of a printed book, so as to verify their number and order'. The operative word is 'verify'. Verify by what? If no bibliographical description of a book is available and no other copy for comparison, 'collation' in this sense can do no more than reveal obvious imperfections.

Yet once the collector has mastered the method in which the leaves of printed books are GATHERED, and the customary SIGNATURE marks by which the gatherings are identified by the printer for the binder, he can at least tell, even where there are no page numerals, whether any leaves are missing from the body of the book. The preliminary leaves are more tricky: for being generally printed last and comprising such variable features as HALF-TITLE, list of contents, dedication, etc., they are not always of straight-forward composition, and often are not signed at all.

But *collation* has acquired a further, and to most collectors more familiar, connotation: the bibliographical description of the physical composition of a book, expressed in a more or less standardised formula. (*Formula*, or *formulary*, is in fact becoming the fashionable term, especially among American bibliographers.) The collation, in this sense, consists of three parts: an indication of the FORMAT, the REGISTER of SIGNATURES, and a record of the number of leaves. Thus '8vo A-L^{8}M^4' means an octavo volume of 92 leaves, gathered in eleven quires of eight leaves and one of four: there is no J (or U or W) in the European signature alphabet, though these letters are sometimes found in 19th century American books. This is an extremely simple example; and in order to show what a collation can look like, here is a notional one published in *The Book Collector* (vol. 1, no. 4) as a test for its bibliographical readers: 'Quarto: $\pi^4 *^2 A^4$B-C^4 (C3 + χ^2) D-G^4 ($\pm$G2) H^4 (-H2.3, =$*^2$).' Dr. Gaskell's expansion of this formula is as follows: 'An unsigned four-leaf section, the first leaf conjugate with the fourth and the second with the third (henceforth a "quarto section"); followed by a conjugate pair of leaves signed with an asterisk; followed by an unsigned quarto section (given the inferential signature A); followed by two quarto sections signed "B" and "C" respectively, in the second of which the third leaf is followed by an inserted unsigned conjugate pair; followed by four quarto sections signed "D", "E", "F" and "G" respectively, in the last of which the second leaf has been removed and replaced with a *cancellans*; followed by a quarto section signed "H", the central conjugate pair of which (i.e. H2.3) was signed with an asterisk, and removed to become the second section of the preliminaries, noted above. (It is assumed that this state of affairs can be proved by the existence of a copy with H2.3 in its original position).' From this it may be seen that the collector who aspires to understand the collation of early books—complicated by HALF-SHEET imposition or gathering, unsigned quires, INSERTED single leaves (or SINGLETONS), CANCELS and so forth—must brace himself to a thorough study of MCKERROW, probably also of Fredson Bowers's *Principles of Bibliographical Description* (1949) and perhaps even of Greg's introduction to vol. IV of *A Bibliography of the English Printed Drama to the Restoration* (1959).

He will note meanwhile certain shorthand conventions; e.g. that P^4 means a four-leaf gathering signed P, whereas P4 (or sometimes P$_4$) means the fourth leaf of the gathering signed P; that the RECTO and VERSO of the leaf are distinguished by some bibliographers as P4^r and P4^v, by others as P4^a and P4^b; that among the older bibliographers unsigned leaves or gatherings are recorded as [P] if the signature letter can be inferred, as [ ] or [-] if it cannot;

that the new school use π for unsigned PRELIMINARY leaves or gatherings, χ for unsigned leaves or gatherings inserted in the body of the book, and an italic letter for an inferential signature. He will further bear in mind that collation takes account only of those leaves of the book which were delivered to the binder by the printer. It includes, that is to say, any BLANK LEAVES or leaves of ADVERTISEMENTS forming part of the gathered sections of the book; but it excludes ENDPAPERS, binder's blanks, inserted advertisements, etc.

It will be seen that collation by signatures, which is the only scientific method of describing the physical make-up of a book, is a technical procedure governed by strict rules. For modern books, however, bibliographers obedient to the DEGRESSIVE principle have evolved various simplified formulæ, more or less adequate to their material but not yet unfortunately (except to some extent in the Soho Bibliographies series) standardised.

COLLECTED

(1) A collected *author* is one who has attracted and retained the attention of book-collectors.

(2) A collected *edition* is the publisher's term for a uniform collective series of an author's works.

(3) A collected *set* is an assemblage of an author's works, not necessarily complete, but implicitly substantial, not necessarily (though often) in first edition, brought together by a collector or bookseller.

(4) A poem, article or short story which had previously appeared in a periodical or anthology is sometimes said to be 'first collected' when it is republished in a volume devoted exclusively to its author's work.

COLONIAL EDITION

It was a common practice in the English publishing trade between the 1880's and the First World War to put up in a different, usually cheaper, style that part of an edition (especially of fiction) which was to be exported for the Empire market. Although they are in PUBLISHER'S

CLOTH, and AS ISSUED, and were usually printed in the same run as the regular edition (though sometimes on different paper), these colonial copies are regarded by collectors with disfavour: cf. LIBRARY BINDINGS, WHOLE-SALERS' BINDINGS.

COLOPHON

The finishing stroke (from the Greek word meaning *summit*): a note at the end of a book (sometimes accompanied by a device or mark) giving all or some of the following particulars: name of work, author, printer, place of printing, date. (See also IMPRINT.) In very early books most of these particulars may not be found elsewhere, and when inspecting the credentials of an INCUNABLE it follows that one begins by turning to the last page, not the first.

In its elementary function of identifying the edition, the colophon has been generally superseded, since the early 16th century, by the title-page; and during the transitional period, when both were in use, discrepancies may be found between the two, when, for instance, a reprinted title-page is combined with an out-dated colophon.

The colophon has persisted to the present day in books whose printer is thought by the publisher (or thinks himself) important enough to justify the formality. And the word is sometimes, but wrongly, used of the printer's—or even of the publisher's—DEVICE on the title-page.

COLOURS OF CLOTH

There has never been much precision or uniformity in describing the colours of cloth used in PUBLISHER's bindings; and unless other bibliographers follow the lead of Messrs. Patrick Cahill (Hilaire Belloc) and R. Toole Stott (W. Somerset Maugham) and the injunctions of Mr. G. Thomas Tanselle (*Virginia Studies*, vol. XXI), this imprecision will no doubt persist. But the resulting mild confusion (e.g. between maroon, plum, claret) is really troublesome only when BINDING VARIANTS are indistinguishable except by colour.

COLOUR-PLATE BOOKS

A broad category, common in booksellers' catalogues, including any book with plates in colour, whether picturesque, sporting or satirical, and whether these are wholly printed in colour, aquatinted with hand-coloured detail or wholly hand-coloured on an engraved or lithographed base (see ILLUSTRATION PROCESSES). Many books in the two last-named classes were originally issued in alternative states—coloured and uncoloured; and a very sharp eye is sometimes needed to distinguish skilful modern colouring from contemporary work.

Despite the existence of technical and descriptive studies by Burch, Martin Hardie, Strange, Dunthorne and others, and the great advance shown in such recent publications as the Abbey Catalogues, the bibliography of colour-plate books is not yet adequate to the specialised complexities of a hybrid form of publishing. The collector who buys them for their looks, or for the subjects portrayed, will usually be content to trust his eye for quality and freshness, his experience or his bookseller for originality, in the colouring. If he is concerned to secure early impressions of the plates he will first take the precaution of checking the dates in their captions with the known date of first publication and also with the date on the title-page; and he will make further comparison with any date which may appear in the WATERMARK of the paper on which the plates are printed. For while the text for a colour-plate book would usually be printed off in a single operation, the plates (being the expensive part) would often be printed—whether or not to be then hand-coloured—in batches as required.

COMMISSION

The term *on commission* is used in two different contexts within our field. Reference may be made, most often in support of an asseveration of rarity, to the fact that a book was *published* on commission. This means that the author paid for it, and the implication is that, if the publisher thought it too bad a risk to take, not many were·printed at the author's risk. This will usually be true, though there have been notable exceptions (e.g. Lewis Carroll, John Ruskin, Bernard Shaw, John Maynard Keynes).

The other use applies to *bidding at auction*: when a bookseller is bidding as agent, he is said to be bidding 'on commission', as distinct from bidding for his own stock (see AUCTIONS (2) Bidding).

CONDITION

'In the purchase of old books', said Dr. Johnson, 'let me recommend to you to examine with great caution whether they are perfect. In the first editions the loss of a leaf is not easily observed'.

After the interest or importance or beauty of the book, which will always be paramount, the two most urgent considerations in the mind of the book-collector are probably (*a*) the rarity of the edition, (*b*) the condition of the copy. And by condition he means a good deal more than the volume's superficial, physical appearance; for the term covers the completeness and integrity of the contents, a proper degree of margin, etc., as well as the beauty or appropriateness or originality, and the state of preservation, of the covering. Thirty years ago Michael Sadleir said: 'The condition of a book must be seen to be realised, and condition more than anything else nowadays dictates value and will continue to dictate it'. On the other hand, Mr. Percy Muir has said: 'I would take an EX-LIBRARY copy rather than none at all'. Somewhere between these two points of view lies the middle way for the average collector.

Each man will adopt his own attitude to this crucial but highly subjective factor, and for the sensible man it will be elastic rather than rigid. But if common sense tells him that he cannot expect to find (or to afford) a fine copy of every book he aspires to possess, so that his decision in an individual case will depend on a combination of taste and judgment, he must nevertheless take some account of book-collecting conventions, as well as bibliographical facts, before he can even determine what 'fine condition' means in a particular context.

'In its absolute sense', as I have suggested elsewhere,[1] 'the term "fine", applied to any book of any period, could be said to mean no more (if no less) than that all its leaves were present, clean, whole and amply margined; that it was sound and undisturbed in its binding; and that that binding, whatever its material, was fresh and unblemished'. This may perhaps serve as a low common denominator. The fastidious collector will apply his own taste and judgment to a number of additional niceties, such as the degree of appropriateness in a binding, and the importance of ORIGINAL leather, cloth, boards or wrappers as compared with merely contemporary covers or with a handsome binding of later date. Yet all but the most determined individualists will pay some attention to the usages ruling among other collectors. The novice of today would soon learn, for instance, that to accept a three-volume novel of post-Regency date in any but its original covers, unless it had some special feature of ASSOCIATION to recommend it, would be a breach of a very rigid convention. He may (as I happen to do) think the convention altogether too rigid; but he must accept its existence.

Anyone but a purist, however, will have to recognise that for very early books, very rare books or simply books he very badly wants, some modifications may have to be made if he is not to resign himself to never possessing a copy at all. Even if he balks at Mr. Muir's ex-library copy, there are occasions when a restored, MADE-UP, REJOINTED, RE-BACKED, CROPPED, WASHED or even RECASED copy may be welcomed to the shelf. The collector should learn enough about the restoration of books to be able to recognise such shortcomings from fine original condition when he sees them; for the exceptions must be very carefully calculated, and nothing is so mortifying as to discover an imperfection in a book which has been on one's shelves for years.

But how, the reader asks, is this connoisseurship of the eye to be applied to a book which is not in the hand but briefly described in the catalogue of a bookseller two hundred miles away? Unless you know from well-tested

[1] *Taste and Technique in Book-Collecting,* chapter XII, 'Condition'.

experience what the bookseller's standards of condition are, and also how to translate into your own terms the descriptive shorthand his cataloguer writes, the answer is to order the book ON APPROVAL if the description of its condition leaves any room for doubt.

Nevertheless, we may take note here of some of the terms commonly used by booksellers in describing the condition of books offered in their catalogues. The adjectives can be roughly grouped under (*a*) descriptive, (*b*) enthusiastic; and only a few of them have been given separate entries in the present book.

(*a*) *Adjectives of Description*

General.—As new, fine, good, fair, satisfactory (a trifle condescending, this), good second-hand condition (i.e. not very good), poor (often coupled with an assurance that the book is very rare in any condition), used, reading copy (fit for nothing more and below collector's standard), working copy (may even need sticking together).

Of exterior.—Fresh, sound (probably lacks 'bloom'), neat (implies sobriety rather than charm); rubbed, scuffed, chafed, tender (of JOINTS), shaken, loose, faded (purple cloth and green leather fade easily), tired (from the French *fatigué*), worn, defective (very widely interpreted), binding copy (i.e. needs it).

Of interior.—Clean, crisp, unpressed, browned (like much later 17th century paper), age-stained, water-stained (usually in the deprecating form, 'a few light waterstains'), foxed (i.e. spotted or discoloured in patches: often 'foxed as usual', implying that practically all copies are), soiled, thumbed (in the more lyrical catalogue-notes, 'lovingly thumbed by an earlier scholar'), and (very rare in English or American catalogues, but commendably frank) washed.

(*b*) *Adjectives of Enthusiasm*

When the condition of a copy is more than merely fine, the superlatives will depend on the cataloguer's taste. A cloth-bound, a boarded or a wrappered book may be called immaculate, mint, pristine, superfine, matchless, superlative, brilliant, in 'Jennings' or 'Parrish' condition (after two notably fastidious collectors of our time); a bound book or set will be handsome, choice (a favourite), elegant, superb, noble, sumptuous, magnificent or the like.

At the other end of the scale, here, under the cheerful headline THE WORST COPY IN THE WORLD, is a New York bookseller's description of a copy (a PRESENTATION copy, it must be added) of a modern first edition: 'shaken, shabby, loose in binding, backstrip broken; foxed and goosed'.

See also ORIGINAL STATE, PUBLISHER'S CLOTH, TRADE BINDING.

CONJUGATE LEAVES

'The leaves which "belong to one another", i.e. if traced into and out of the back of the book, are found to form a *single* piece of paper, are said to be "conjugate" ' (MCKERROW). The conjugacy of leaves derives from the form in which the printed SHEET is folded. For instance, in an octavo book, the first and eighth, the second and seventh leaves (and so on) of each GATHERING will be conjugate. (*The leaf under the reader's right hand* E3, *is conjugate with* E6, *which comprises pages* 75 *and* 76.)

The most frequent occasions for the use of this term are in connexion with HALF-TITLE or TITLE leaves or other PRELIMS, initial or terminal BLANKS, leaves of ADVERTISEMENTS, CANCELS, etc.; i.e. those whose bibliographical relationship to other leaves in the volume may be in doubt. Non-conjugate leaves are sometimes called SINGLETONS.

CONTEMPORARY

The presence of this desirable attribute—in binding, in annotations or ownership entries, in the colouring of illustrations, etc.—is less often susceptible of actual proof or even reasonable certainty than one might suppose from the freedom with which it is claimed by cataloguers. In its application to bindings, however, the term is by general agreement interpreted fairly broadly: anything in the style of the decade, or even of the quarter-century if before 1700, being accepted as contemporary.

For the question of contemporary colouring in engravings, etc., see COLOUR-PLATE BOOKS.

COPYRIGHT EDITIONS

This term has one specialised use which concerns the collector. In order to safeguard copyright by formal publication (whether of a poem printed in a magazine, or to comply with the American law, or for some other reason), a small number of copies of a pamphlet or book may have been printed before the regular edition, and formally 'published' but not distributed or sold in the ordinary way. Familiar examples are Swinburne *Siena* 1868, the suppressed portion of Wilde *De Profundis* 1913, and a number of pieces by Kipling.

COPYRIGHT LIBRARIES

Under the Copyright Act of 1911, publishers are bound to deliver a copy of every book published in the United Kingdom to the British Museum; also, if called upon to do so, to the National Libraries of Scotland and Wales, the University libraries of Oxford and Cambridge, and Trinity College, Dublin. This obligation, in one form or another, dates back to the 17th century (the Royal Library, Oxford and Cambridge were provided for by the Licensing Act of 1662), but it is only in comparatively recent years, since its performance was systematised, that the delivery of these copyright, or *statutory*, copies on, or very near to, publication day became the rule rather than the exception. Where —but only where—this presumption is sustained by the recorded date of reception, the statutory copies provide useful, and nowadays often cited, evidence of an early ISSUE or a PRIMARY BINDING in doubtful cases.

(See also REGISTER.)

The procedure in U.S.A. is different and more consistently useful to bibliographers: deposit and registration with the Library of Congress being prerequisite to the legal recognition of copyright.

COTTAGE STYLE
(OF BINDING)

A style of decoration in which the top and bottom of the rectangular PANEL, which itself will be filled with smaller ornaments in a variety of rich designs, slope away from a broken centre, thus producing a sort of gabled effect—what architects call a broken pediment. The cottage style was popular with binders of the last forty years of the 17th century (some of the finest examples being credited to Samuel Mearne's workshop) and it was still being used on pocket almanacs and prayer-books as late as the 1770s.

COURTESY BOOKS

This class of books has been defined as follows by one of its chief proponents: 'Manuals setting forth rules and standards for the education, and instruction in polite and correct behaviour, of a Gentleman, based originally on the teaching in the Italian princely academies, and gaining an increasingly wide acceptance and popularity in the 17th and 18th centuries (Prototype: Castiglione's *Il Cortegiano*, 1528).'

COVER, COVERS

The upper cover is the front, the lower the back side of the binding: upper and lower being preferable terms, as avoiding possible confusion with *back* when used in the sense of SPINE. In the plural, the term is used in such phrases as 'covers fresh, interior slightly spotted', 'loose in covers but a clean copy'; or occasionally 'covers detached', which means that the sides are off but present.

The phrase, 'covers in' or 'covers preserved', in conjunction with the description of a leather or half-leather binding, means that the original cloth, stripped from its boards, has been bound in, usually at the end. This was a not uncommon practice during the period (*c.* 1890–1920) when respect for original condition was becoming established as an article of faith, but had not yet overcome the

Victorian and gentlemanly view that any book worth keeping deserved binding. Resort to it often implies that the cloth was in mediocre condition, and it is at best an unsatisfactory compromise.

French binders, since the late 19th century, have almost invariably bound in the printed wrappers of any book of bibliophile interest.

CRISP

Of the leaves of a book—brisk in texture, unpressed; of paper boards—unthumbed, not dulled with handling, having something of the original nap still upon them; of publisher's cloth—fresh of fabric (even if faded in colour), with the gilding bright, the BLOCKING unsubdued, the edges and corners of the covers sharp.

CROPPED

Of margins, cut down by the binder's knife, usually seriously: nowadays a slightly old-fashioned, but still pointed and vigorous, alternative to *cut down*, *cut into*, *short*; e.g. 'a cropped copy', 'SIDE-NOTE on p. 61 cropped as usual' or 'a few HEADLINES cropped'. These terms mean that the binder's incursion into the actual printed matter has gone farther than mere SHAVING: he has cut off whole letters if not words. Thus, in 'a short copy' one expects very little margin at head or tail, but one assumes that if HEADLINES, page numerals or CATCHWORDS were cut into, the cataloguer would say so. Of 'a cropped copy' one would have little right to complain even if the text itself proved to be cut into.

CRUSHED MOROCCO

MOROCCO leather which has been so thoroughly ironed, pressed or rolled that the grain of the original skin has been almost obliterated. This is done in the piece, not when it is on the boards. The characteristic high polish is given after the volume is bound.

CUIR-CISELÉ

'Decoration of the book-cover by cutting the design in the leather instead of the more normal TOOLING or STAMPING.' (J. P. Harthan.)

CURIOSA, CURIOUS

This familiar subject-heading may cover anything from the risqué or gallant, which might equally well be classed as FACETIÆ, to the indecent, which would be more properly listed under *Erotica*. It will sometimes include medical or pathological works, but these are nowadays mostly catalogued frankly under 'Sex' or more genteelly under 'Sexology'.

CUTS

A good, old-fashioned, omnibus word, meaning illustrations printed with the text (as distinct from PLATES), whether from wood or metal, and whether cut or engraved.

DECKLE EDGES

The rough, untrimmed edges of a sheet of hand-made paper (the *deckle* being the frame or band which confines it in manufacture). Much prized by collectors, especially in books before the age of EDITION-BINDING in cloth, as tangible evidence that the leaves are UNCUT; for the deckle edge normally would be—and indeed was meant to be—trimmed off by the binder.

In modern books deckle edges are an affectation, mainly (but not, alas, entirely) confined to PRESS BOOKS, LIMITED EDITIONS, etc. They have, certainly, a sort of antiquarian charm, even though they can nowadays be artificially produced in machine-made papers; but they collect dust and, being technically obsolete for a century, hardly avoid a self-conscious air. In books of reference they are intolerable.

DECKLE-FETISHISM

The over-zealous, undiscriminating (and often very expensive) passion for uncut edges in books which were intended to have their edges cut.

See UNCUT, TRADE BINDING, EDITION-BINDING.

DEDICATION COPY

It is customary for an author to present an early copy of his book to the person (if any) to whom it is dedicated. This is known as the *dedication copy*; and it will rank very high, in the estimation of most collectors, among PRESENTATION or ASSOCIATION copies of the book.

The term cannot properly be applied, as it sometimes is, to a copy which merely bears the signature or bookplate of the dedicatee, since he (or she) may well have bought an extra copy or copies of the book.

DEFECTIVE

Used by cataloguers to cover almost every degree of defectiveness, more often of the exterior than of the interior of a book. Thus, a copy described as having 'backstrip defective', may prove to have either just a small chip out of the top or practically no back left at all.

DEGRESSIVE BIBLIOGRAPHY

The degressive principle was formulated by Falconer Madan in a memorandum subjoined to Pollard and Greg's classic paper, 'Some Points in Bibliographical Descriptions' (Bibliographical Society, 1909, reprinted 1950). It is 'the principle of varying a description according to the difference of the period treated or of the importance of the work to be described'. Newtonian in its simplicity, Einsteinian in its weight, it has yet to penetrate the consciousness of our more pachydermatous bibliographers.

DENTELLE

A binder's term (from the French = lace) meaning a border with a lacy pattern on the inner edge, usually gilt. *Dentelle* decoration may be used on the outside of the covers; but in bindings of the past hundred years or so it has been more often used, in a somewhat emasculated form, on the inside —usually described as *inside dentelles*.

DEVICE

From the earliest days (Fust and Schoeffer, 1457) many printers used a device, or 'printer's mark', to accompany—

or occasionally to serve as—their IMPRINT in a book. These will be found along with the COLOPHON at the end of books printed before 1500–10, and thereafter more usually on the title-page. Familiar examples are the Aldine Anchor and Dolphin, the Tree of Knowledge of the Estiennes, the Globe of the Elzevirs, Day's Sun and, later, the Clarendon Press's engraving of the Sheldonian Theatre and the Cambridge University Press's figure of Charity.

Although the practice declined towards the end of the 17th century, it has never died out. And as it was adopted by publishers as well as printers when the two trades began to be distinct, the publisher's device or mark is today the commoner of the two. Among the most distinguished of contemporary designs are the Borzoi of Alfred A. Knopf and the Reynard of Rupert Hart-Davis. (*See the title-page and p. 211 of this book for one or the other.*)

DIAPER

A term used in descriptions of bindings. As applied to decoration in gold or BLIND on leather bindings, it is essentially a repetitive pattern of small diamonds or lozenges.

When used of PUBLISHER'S CLOTH bindings it refers to the grain of the fabric itself: a cross-hatched effect of lozenges, diamonds or occasionally triangles. Diaper cloths were popular in the late 1830's and the 1840's, and have remained standard fabrics, in one form or another, ever since.

DICED

A binder's term, meaning ruled or stamped into a pattern of diamond squares. RUSSIA is often diced, MOROCCO hardly ever. Diced CALF was common in the first quarter of the 19th century, but has been uncommon since. Diced fabrics for PUBLISHER'S CLOTH (a bolder form of DIAPER) were popular between 1835 and 1845.

DISBOUND

Obsolete since the 17th century, this term has now been usefully revived (first by John Hayward in the Rothschild

DISBOUND (continued)

Catalogue, 1954) to describe those books or pamphlets which have been torn out of composite volumes. (The common term UNBOUND is imprecise, for it can be applied to a book that has never been bound.)

This practice, which is on the increase, is convenient for the bookseller who hopes to sell one rare pamphlet out of a volume, but would jettison the rest; and sometimes also to the collector who has no wish to encumber his shelves with matter extraneous to his interest. But it is strongly disapproved by purists, since it destroys a bibliophilic, if not a bibliographical, entity; erases evidence of an earlier owner's taste and even his identity; and sacrifices an old (if not always a contemporary) binding and appearance in favour of a new and often less congenial one.

DOCTORED

Restored, repaired, rebuilt: a blunter and less elastic term than SOPHISTICATED, but like it always used in a pejorative sense, and so seldom appearing in a bookseller's catalogue except in the negative, e.g.' Binding shabby and lacks the leaf of advertisements, but an entirely undoctored copy of this rare book'.

DIVINITY CALF

An unpleasant kind of smooth calf, usually of a colour between lavender and cocoa, much favoured by mid-19th century binders for theological or devotional books, especially when rebinding a volume of earlier date. Other common features of the divinity style are BEVELLED boards, red edges and a design of what are known as 'Oxford' rules (a PANEL in which the four component lines are extended beyond their intersections) in BLIND or black: whence sometimes known as 'Oxford style'.

DIVISIONAL TITLE

A separate title-page for a section or division of a book; cf. GENERAL TITLE.

DOS-À-DOS BINDING

'A term not used by the French [cf. *demi-tasse*] who speak of *une reliure jumelle*. The twin volumes are usually two small service books or works of piety. They are bound together, not one after the other, but in such a way that they share a common lower board, with the volumes upside down to each other and their fore-edges facing in opposite directions. Their upper boards, usually covered with gold-tooled leather or embroidered work, form the outer covers. Thus, whichever way the twin binding is picked up it opens at one or other title-page'. (H. M. Nixon.)

DOUBLURE, DOUBLÉ

A binder's term, meaning that the PASTE-DOWN (or inside lining of the covers) is not of paper but of leather, usually decorated. Since *doublures* have always been much commoner in French bindings than in English, there is no English word for them.

DRAWER-HANDLE TOOL (or DECORATION)

The 'drawer-handle' TOOL, commonly used in groups or sequences, was popular with binders of the Restoration period (foreign as well as English). Its name is presumably supposed to be self-explanatory: actually, it looks more like the standard decorative unit of an Ionic capital than the handle of a drawer.

DROPPED HEAD

A printer's term, restricted for our purposes almost exclusively to the phrase 'drop title' or 'dropped-head title', which means that there is no title-page, the title being placed at the head of the first page of text; chiefly applicable to pamphlets, leaflets, etc. In America this is sometimes called a *caption title*.

DROPPED LETTERS AND NUMERALS

Among the minor accidents to which type on the printing press is prone, none is commoner than that the inking apparatus pulls out or askew a loose letter (or numeral). The result, on the printed page, is called a dropped letter. Sometimes the fault is not noticed, so that the first copies printed off are perfect and later ones faulty. Sometimes the fault is noticed during the run, the machine stopped,

DROPPED LETTERS (continued)

the type replaced: making three STATES of the IMPRESSION, the first and third being probably indistinguishable. In other cases the loose type falls out before printing actually starts. This means that the first copies run off will show a dropped letter, while later ones, if the fault is noticed and rectified, will be perfect. (*Here are two dr pp*e*d letters.*)

It follows that anyone—bibliographer, bookseller's cataloguer or collector—who thinks to determine priority between two states of an impression or edition solely on the evidence of dropped letters is (to put it charitably) an optimist. And when the collector sees, as he often will, some modern first edition described as 'first issue, with the dropped letter on page 163', he may be excused for demanding chapter and verse, not only for this, but for any other bibliographical *dicta* in the vicinity.

DUODECIMO (12mo, 12°)

A duodecimo, commonly called a twelvemo, is a small size of book, between octavo and sixteenmo, about the size of a Penguin or slightly smaller.

For details see FORMAT.

DUST-JACKET (or DUST-WRAPPER)

The paper jacket, more or less adorned, which is wrapped round most modern books to protect the cloth covers in transit between the publisher and the reader. Dust-*jacket* is a preferable term to dust-*wrapper*, since it avoids the chance of confusion with WRAPPERS.

The earliest recorded dust-jacket dates from 1832 (many decades earlier than most people would guess). But its history till the end of the century is almost entirely unexplored, and surviving examples earlier than the mideighties are very uncommon indeed. This is natural enough, since dust-jackets were—and functionally still are —*ephemera* in the most extreme sense: wrappings intended to be thrown away *before* the objects they were designed to accompany were put to use.

Until about fifty years ago, therefore, it would probably be true to say that any dust-jacket that had survived had done so by accident—by the omission to discard, not by any conscious intention to preserve. Exceptions would have been provided by those mildly eccentric people who keep everything wrapped up; but not (in England at any rate) by any statutory preservation, since not being prints or pictures they were no concern of museums, and not being part of the book they were, and are, normally jettisoned by librarians.

With the great resurgence of collecting MODERN FIRSTS in the 1920's, however, dust-jackets of all kinds came into their own with a vengeance. For whereas no one knows whether *Eric or Little by Little* (1858) or *The Prisoner of Zenda* (1894) was issued in one, any book published since the turn of the century was plausibly assumed to have been. And as the insistence on a high standard of condition became increasingly widespread, it seemed logical to demand, of a recent book described as 'mint' or 'as new', that it should still be in its original jacket, whether this was of any intrinsic interest or not.

That this insistence sometimes became rather hysterical is true. Yet dust-jackets may be of artistic interest; they may have an illustration not in the book itself. They may contain a 'blurb' written by the author (admittedly not usually easy to identify), or preliminary comments by critics of distinction. They nowadays normally contain biographical information about the author and often a photograph; sometimes bibliographical details of his other books. How many jackets for Messrs. Faber and Faber's volumes of poetry had 'blurbs' written by T. S. Eliot, for many years one of the firm's directors? Professors Tanselle and Gallup, among others, have of late years spoken up for the recognition of the jacket as, in biblio-graphical terms, an integral component of the modern book: the former's paper to the Bibliographical Society (*The Library*, June 1971) entitled 'Book-Jackets, Blurbs and Bibliographers' is, indeed, the most comprehensive as well as the most persuasive study of the book-jacket published to date. In consequence it is probable that today most serious collectors in this field are willing to pay the premium that booksellers normally charge for its presence.

They need to remember, however, that since the
marriage of book and dust-jacket was never meant to be
permanent, divorces can all too easily be followed by re-
marriages; and it may take a shrewd eye to tell, without
external evidence, whether the jacket on a modern first
edition has always been on it or came from another copy.
Often this may be no great matter. But did it perhaps
come from a later edition? Anyway, one should never be
so dazzled by a clean dust-jacket as to omit scrutiny of the
cloth beneath it; for once in a while the alien character of
the former will be exposed by the fact that the latter is
quite shabby.

EARLY PRINTED

Fifty years ago this would have meant, to most collectors,
INCUNABULA: that is, books printed in the 15th century.
Thirty years ago it would have included POST-INCUNAB-
ULA. Today, if a man says he collects early printed books
he generally means that his interest is bounded by the
year 1600 or thereabouts. For English books—though the
term is mostly applied to books collected as printing rather
than for their contents, and is therefore more often used
of Continental books—the category may extend to 1640.
This was the last year before the abolition of the Star
Chamber, which had gagged English printing, and a date
which has become a bibliographical landmark (rather like
1500), as the end of the span covered by the SHORT-TITLE
CATALOGUE.

Some booksellers, however, interpret the term a good
deal more liberally when listing a group of books under
this heading in a catalogue. This will in one case be due to
the cataloguer genuinely considering that 1695, say, is
'early'; and since time is a relative thing, who shall contra-
dict him? In another, it may possibly be that he cannot see
any interest of author or subject in the book, but hopes
that the label 'early printed' will help to sell it.

EDGES

Unless specifically qualified (e.g. GILT TOPS), this refers to
the three outer edges of the leaves, which may be UNCUT

(or cut), TRIMMED, GILT, GAUFFRED, SPRINKLED, stained
(usually red or yellow: in Irish books of the second half of
the 18th century sometimes green or blue), MARBLED or
(rarely—a French style) GILT ON THE ROUGH.

EDITIO PRINCEPS

Latin for *first edition*. Purists restrict the use of the term to
the first printed edition of a work which was in circulation
in manuscript before printing was invented. It is common
usage for any first edition of a classical author. There is old
and respectable precedent for its use in a wider sense,
simply as a synonym for first edition; but this is apt to
sound a trifle affected today.

EDITION AND IMPRESSION

Strictly speaking, an *edition* comprises all copies of a book
printed at *any* time or times from one setting-up of type
without substantial change (including copies printed from
STEREOTYPE, electrotype or similar plates made from that
setting of type); while an *impression* comprises the whole
number of copies of that edition printed at *one* time, i.e.
without the type or plates being removed from the press.

In most books before 1750 the two terms in effect mean
the same thing, for the printer normally distributed his
type as soon as possible after it had been printed from; and
if more copies were wanted he reset it, thus creating a new
edition. In those days labour was cheap, type metal expensive and printing presses few to a business. In the third
quarter of the century, however, London printers began to
reprint best-sellers from standing type, usually several
impressions in quick succession; and indeed at all periods
new impressions have often been described in imprints
and advertisements as new editions.

With the increase of mechanisation in the nineteenth
century practice moved steadily towards the modern
system, whereby type or plates are kept 'standing' (as the
phrase is) in case reprints are called for; and the *edition*, in
its strict sense, might therefore be subdivided into a number of different *impressions*, which might or might not

be adequately differentiated. Thus a 'tenth impression' printed from the same type-setting five years after the first, would still be part of the first edition—and so, for the matter of that, as Professor Bowers and other pundits have warned us, would a photo-lithographic or xerographic off-set impression printed five hundred years after the first.

This presents the first edition collector with a prospect of the most frightful anomalies—in theory. And sometimes, it is true, the difficulties are real ones both to him and still more to the bibliographer. But the majority of these are solved in advance, for all but pedants, by the sensible convention that *first edition*, unless qualified in some way, shall be deemed to mean *first impression of the first edition.* This has been taken for granted for so many years that it hardly needs saying. And the term *impression*, in the sense here discussed (see IMPRESSION for others), seldom needs to be used at all by the ordinary cataloguer.

See also ISSUES AND STATES.

EDITION-BINDING

Wholesale quantity binding (actually almost always CASING) to the order and at the expense of the publisher or distributor, as opposed to individual binding executed for the retail bookseller or the purchaser.

ÉDITION DE LUXE

Any book produced to be admired for its appearance rather than read qualifies for the description *édition de luxe*, and a good many others have had it applied to them for the not necessarily relevant reason that they were issued in a LIMITED EDITION. It is appropriate that we use a French phrase, because the French have been, since the 17th century, past masters in the production of such books, which have always held the place of honour in French collecting taste.

The *édition de luxe* is as old as printing. In the 15th century a certain number of copies of any imposing book would sometimes be printed on VELLUM; Aldus Manutius of Venice might print a few copies on blue paper; 'fine paper' copies, at a higher price, were common enough among 17th and 18th century books (see THICK PAPER) and LARGE PAPER COPIES have been established luxuries for the past three centuries. Of illustrated books, some copies will often have been printed with the plates in proof state or on a special paper. And from the 1890s onwards many *éditions de luxe* have been signed by their authors or illustrators.

When W. Carew Hazlitt said, in 1904, that the *édition de luxe* was 'dilettantism *in extremis*', he was reacting rather crustily to a then recent craze for limited *de luxe* editions of books by contemporary writers, which he regarded as merely a method of fleecing credulous collectors. While it is not true that all such productions are bait for suckers, it is true that the phrase has been used to dignify a large number of shoddily pretentious books published at fancy prices. And since these prices are by no means always maintained in the realistic arena of the second-hand market, the novice collector will do well to cock a sceptical eye at any book which seems to have nothing but 'E.D.L.' to recommend it.

EDWARDS OF HALIFAX

The Edwards family (William and five sons, of whom James was the ablest) were booksellers and publishers as well as binders, but it is in this last capacity that they qualify for a separate entry in this book because they had three specialities popular with collectors, examples of which, therefore, are likely to be attributed to 'Edwards of Halifax' even when (as almost invariably) unsigned. These specialities were FORE-EDGE PAINTING, a technique revived and popularised by William and continued particularly by Thomas; the ETRUSCAN style of decorating CALF, if not evolved by William, at least very early and successfully adopted by him; and a process, patented by James in 1785, for rendering VELLUM transparent and painting or drawing designs on the under-side, so that when used for decorating the covers of a volume they were protected from wear and tear.

EDWARDS OF HALIFAX (continued)

All three specialities seem to have been carried on both in the Edwards's home town of Halifax, where Thomas was in business until 1826, and in London, where James and John opened a bookshop in Pall Mall in 1784 and Richard another in Bond Street in 1792. But regardless of its place of origin, any binding of the period which approximates in style to any one of the three specialities (not to mention many a vellum binding with blue LETTER-ING-PIECES and key-pattern gilt tooling in the prevailing neo-classical style) is apt to be attributed to *Edwards of Halifax*.

ELSE FINE

A favourite phrase with the never-say-die type of cata-loguer: used in such contexts as 'somewhat wormed and age-stained, piece torn from title, headlines cut into, joints repaired, new lettering-piece, else fine'. I once saw 'second impression, else fine'.

EMBLEM BOOKS

A specialised type of illustrated book popular in the 16th and 17th centuries. The emblem was a woodcut or en-graving giving pictorial expression to a moral fable or allegory and interpreted by a motto, epigram, or brief sentence. One of the first to be published in England was *A choice of emblemes* by Geoffrey Whitney, 1586; the most famous, Benlowes *Theophila* 1652.

EMBLEMATICAL

Used to describe appropriate ornaments or symbols on leather bindings; e.g. hunting horns for Surtees, eagles for Napoleonica, harps for Ireland.

EMBROIDERED BINDINGS

Bindings embroidered with elaborate designs were cert-ainly put on MS service books in mediæval times, though hardly any English examples have survived. There are plenty of 16th century specimens, some of them with a royal PROVENANCE; but their heyday was the first half of the 17th century. Some of these are plainly amateur work, but the majority were undoubtedly executed by professional embroiderers. They are usually called *needlework bindings*.

ENDPAPERS, ENDLEAVES

With rare exceptions, endpapers are not part of the book as printed. They are the double leaves added at front and back by the binder, the outer leaf of each being pasted to the inner surface of the cover (known as the *paste-down*), the inner leaves (or *free endpapers*) forming the first and last of the volume when bound or CASED. Occasionally (in very cheap books since about 1880, in some war-time 'economy' publications, and in certain modern PRIVATE PRESS books) blank leaves of the first or last section have been used as endpapers. The technical term for this is *own ends*.

Leather-bound and vellum-bound books of the 16th and 17th centuries sometimes had no endpapers. For leather and half leather bindings, MARBLED endpapers have been used since the late 17th century. In EDITION-BOUND books of the second half of the 19th century they were often of slightly shiny paper; usually tinted (though white on the underside, i.e. the inner-facing pages of the free endpapers); sometimes patterned; occasionally printed with publisher's advertisements. In modern books they may carry maps, genealogical trees, illustrations, etc. In more elaborate leather bindings they may be of silk or some other special material, when they are called LININGS or liners. In really sumptuous bindings the paste-down may be replaced by a DOUBLURE of leather.

ENGRAVINGS

Illustrations or decorations printed (intaglio) from a metal plate, or (in relief) from the end-grain of a wood-block, whose surface has been incised with a graver or burin. The metal was usually copper from the late 15th century until about 1830, when steel began to be used.

See also ILLUSTRATION PROCESSES, WOOD-CUT.

ERASURES

The commonest occasions for erasure are names or other inscriptions on half-title or title (usually legible under ultra-violet light): often clumsily effected by a previous owner (perhaps ashamed of parting with the book), but sometimes with more care by, or for, a collector or book-seller willing to sacrifice evidence of PROVENANCE for a clean page. If the erasure is about the size and shape of a penny piece, the odds are that its object was a library or personal stamp. Erasures (usually made with very great care) near the centre of the title-page, or in modern books in the upper part of its reverse side, invite suspicion. There is always the possibility that the words removed were not written but printed, and that they may have been *Second* (or *nth*) *Edition* (or *Impression*).

ERRATA

Mistakes and misprints discovered after the book has been printed; also called *corrigenda*, and in some early books by the homely name of 'faults escaped'. If the errors are noticed before the PRELIMS have been completed (these being customarily printed last), there is sometimes a spare page or part of a page to accommodate them. If not, they may be printed on a slip, or on an extra leaf, to be TIPPED IN when the book is bound. The same method is used for dealing with *addenda* (things to be added). When a book was published in several volumes appearing at intervals, later volumes sometimes contained lists of errata or addenda for the earlier.

It sometimes happens that the errors are not detected until after the book has been published, so that early copies will already have been issued when the decision to print an errata slip or leaf is taken. But it is only rarely that docu-mentary evidence exists to prove this one way or the other; and since errata slips, by their nature, are liable to accidental omission or detachment, they pose a frequent problem to collectors. For, of a book in which an errata slip is some-times found, is he to consider that a copy without it is incomplete? Or is he justified in concluding, if there is no sign that it ever contained one, that this copy was issued before the slip was printed?

In default of external evidence, judgment can only be empirical. Where the large majority of recorded copies contain an errata slip or leaf (e.g. Gibbon *Decline and Fall* 1776, Bulwer Lytton *The Last Days of Pompeii* 1834) its absence will be considered an imperfection. Where one is seldom found, or where it is absent from presentation copies or copies with early inscriptions, the presumption is that it was printed after publication—e.g. Copernicus *De Revolutionibus Orbium Cælestium* 1543.

A further complication is introduced when additiona errors are noticed after an errata slip has been printed, necessitating an enlarged list—e.g. Keats *Endymion* 1820, which sometimes has a slip with a one-line *erratum*, sometimes five lines of *errata*, and sometimes both; but, being hardly ever found without any at all, is usually thought to require one. Of Sir Thomas Browne *Urne Buriall and the Garden of Cyrus* 1658 on the other hand, three ISSUES are tentatively distinguished: (1) the commonest, without errata; (2) much less common, with an errata slip of 18 lines; and (3) very rare indeed on present evidence, with a slip containing 24 lines of errata.

In some books, moreover, though the errors and misprints were corrected during printing, errata slips or leaves were, nevertheless, provided for the whole edition, for the benefit of any copies which might contain even partially uncorrected text. Of such books (e.g. Fielding *Tom Jones* 1749) it is customary to prefer those copies which have both the errata and a completely uncorrected text.

Booksellers are naturally disposed to make the best of their offerings; and unless they have been given a ruling by the bibliographers, the catalogue note may read either 'complete with the errata slip', or 'early issue, without the errata'.

ESTEEMED

This term, applied to an author or an edition, was once a great favourite with booksellers, and it may still be found in catalogues of traditional style. It means, in effect, 'collected', and suggests that whatever the author's standing may be among readers or literary critics, he has been canonised by book-collectors. When used, as often, of an author who was once fashionable but is so no longer, its intention (however unconscious) is something between an incantation and a threat: designed to persuade humble or credulous collectors that if so-and-so has been collected by others, it is their duty to follow suit.

ET INFRA

This phrase, which is latin for *and below*, is used in describing a collection or set of books not all of the same size. For instance, '74 vols., 8vo *et infra*' means that the largest volumes are of octavo size, while others are 12mo and/or smaller.

ETRUSCAN STYLE

(OF BINDING)

Defined by Oldham as 'the decoration of calf bindings by means of acid staining, with classical ornament, e.g. Greek vases, palmettes, Greek key pattern, etc. usually as a border round a plain TREE-CALF PANEL [though a central ornament, such as a figure, is not uncommon]; some simple gold TOOLING was sometimes combined with the staining, which was usually in terra-cotta and black'.

The style was a speciality of EDWARDS OF HALIFAX and seems to have been invented either by them or their contemporary John Whitaker. It was popular during the period of the 'classical revival' in the other decorative arts —say 1785–1820.

EVANS

American Bibliography, A Chronological Dictionary of all Books, Pamphlets and Periodical Publications printed in the United States from 1639 to 1820, by Charles Evans, 13 volumes, 1903–55 (vol. 13 by C. K. Shipton), Index 1959 and Supplement 1970 by R. P. Bristol.

Frequently quoted simply by number. (cf. SABIN, BLANCK)

An adverb of enthusiasm, frequently and irritatingly mis-used with the adjective *rare*. Rarity may be extreme, notorious, ultimate, even legendary; but it cannot be excessive.

EX-LIBRARY

This term is used of a book which has at one time been in a lending library. Even in pre-cloth days the libraries some-times identified their property by a printed label pasted on the inside or outside of the front cover; and in books of this date which are otherwise in good order such labels are regarded with tolerance by collectors and by bibliographers with relish. It was in the second half of the 19th century that the practice of sticking large labels on the outside front cover became really common; and novels, being intended mainly for borrowers not buyers, are particularly liable to have been thus disfigured. W. H. Smith and some other English libraries pasted their labels inside; and these, though they will normally be mentioned by the cataloguer, are viewed more leniently, if the copy is otherwise clean and sound, which ex-library copies seldom are.

But for cloth books, whether *outside* labels have been left in place or whether, as often with books of any con-sequence, they have been removed, their presence or traces are regarded with lively disfavour by most experienced collectors and with contempt by the fastidious. Ex-library copies will be admitted only when experience has proved that no better copy can reasonably be expected—or, of course, afforded.

When an expert job has been made of the removal of library labels, which often means RE-CASING the book, it is not always easy to detect their traces. But even if the tell-tale signs of re-casing are absent, the rectangular scars left by the labels of Mr. Mudie, or the smaller shield-shaped scars inherited by more modern books from Messrs. Boots, will often have had to be touched up to match the rest of the front cover. And even if this is not betrayed by a generally over-varnished air or an imperfect adjustment of colour, the marks are almost always visible when the book is held at an angle in a good light.

EX-LIBRIS
See BOOK-PLATE

EXTENDED

(1) When used of individual leaves, this means that the inner margin has been renewed (cf. RE-MARGINED): an operation more often necessary with title-leaves, frontispieces, plates, maps and final leaves than elsewhere in the book, since these will be the leaves most likely to have come loose and consequently got frayed or otherwise damaged at the inner edge. Occasionally, however, if a book has to be MADE-UP from a narrower copy, the alien leaves may be extended at the inner margin so that their outer edges range with those of their neighbours.

(2) As applied to a whole volume or volumes—see EXTRA-ILLUSTRATED.

EXTRA
(OF BINDING)

A binder's term for a copy which has been bound and 'finished' (i.e. lettered and decorated) in the most elegant style (saving, of course, *super-extra*), with all edges gilt and usually a good deal of gilt decoration. While applicable to any kind of leather, it is used chiefly of MOROCCO bindings.

EXTRA-ILLUSTRATED

In 1769 James Granger published a *Biographical History of England* with blank leaves for the addition of portraits, etc., to the taste of the purchaser. Hence *grangerising*, for the practice which he formalised and promoted. Grangerised or extra-illustrated books, as they are now more commonly called, are copies which have had added to them, either by a private owner or professionally, engraved portraits, prints, etc., usually cut out of other books, and sometimes also autograph letters, documents or drawings.

Frequently plates have to be INLAID in larger paper to match the size of the volume. Occasionally a whole book, originally of smallish format, has its text inlaid throughout, in order that plates of larger format can be inserted without folding. Sometimes two or three volumes will be 'extended' to as many as eight or ten.

There is no hard-and-fast border-line between a modestly extra-illustrated book and a book which could equally well be described as having 'a number of interesting portraits inserted'. But one might say that, for a copy to qualify, the additional matter would have to be sufficiently ample to necessitate rebinding, with extra leaves.

EXTRACT

As a noun, this is used of papers, articles, stories, etc., taken out of periodicals, transactions of learned societies or the like and listed individually. Sometimes called *excerpts*.

See also DISBOUND, OFFPRINT.

FACETIÆ

A subject-heading in booksellers' catalogues whose connotation varies widely. In addition to jest-books and oddities, it may include works which another would list under CURIOSA or even *Erotica*. But it is used for the milder of this kind of fare, and it retains a nuance of lightness or gaiety: Balzac's *Droll Stories* certainly, Boccaccio permissibly, *The History of the Rod* inappropriately, and certainly not Krafft-Ebing.

FACSIMILES AND FAKES

A facsimile is defined by SOED as 'an exact copy, counterpart or representation'. It figures frequently in the nightmares of collectors, causes booksellers more trouble than almost any other factor in their business, and has been known to upset the studious equanimity of librarians. For an exact copy is a menacing thing to those who pursue originals.

At one time and another facsimiles have been made, with the most admirable intentions, of autograph letters, documents, broadsides, proclamations, maps, issues of newspapers, and printed books. These legitimate facsimiles may be made by photolithography or by one of the many other photographic processes. (There is also the so-called 'type-facsimile': a reprint that follows the original as faithfully as it can with the type and paper available, but makes no pretence to exact imitation.) Some of these facsimiles are good, some bad, many indifferent. Their producers sometimes have and sometimes have not, indicated indelibly on them that they *are* facsimiles. When they have, it has sometimes been on the cover or on an additional leaf, which can be detached. Even clumsy facsimiles may deceive the inexperienced. The deception is usually, though not of course always, independent of assistance from a third party. A good facsimile may deceive even a moderately experienced eye at first sight, if it is of something the eye's owner did not know had ever been facsimiled and if it is found in respectable company.

If there is, or has been, intent to deceive; if a facsimile of a pamphlet, say, has been carefully discoloured, treated with tea and heat, or otherwise given a plausible appearance of age; and if it is carefully placed among, or even bound up with, the sort of neighbours its original would have had, then its true character may be very difficult to detect. There is a story (doubtless apocryphal) that a very carefully doctored copy of a facsimile of *The Compleat Angler* (1653) was once passed as genuine, after the most scrupulous examination, by the authorities of the British Museum itself.

But once the slightest suspicion is aroused as to the genuineness of a piece of printing, the odds against a facsimile of a whole book or pamphlet surviving rigorous scrutiny are enormous. 'Easy as it appears to be', said Thomas J. Wise, 'to fabricate reprints of rare books, it is in actual practice absolutely impossible to do so in such a manner that detection cannot follow the result.' Even with the reservation implicit in 'cannot', this may seem a trifle sweeping to anyone who has been bitten. But it is true. For whereas autograph letters, drawings, etc., being unique, can be *invented* by a skilful *forger* (indeed, even printed books can be invented, as Wise himself demonstrated), a facsimile presupposes an original, with which it can be compared. With something very rare or unique, the comparison may be a laborious task, but it will be obligatory where there is doubt of authenticity. And, with the necessary margin for human fallibility, it may be said that no facsimile will stand comparison with its original.

By far the commonest and most deceptive kind of facsimile, however, is one supplied to make good an imperfect
book: whether of a leaf or two, part of a torn page, or even
a few words. 'Where such insertion takes the form of an
honest and unconcealed facsimile from another copy of the
same edition,' wrote MCKERROW, 'it is clear gain, for none
but the most uncompromising of bibliographical purists
would prefer an imperfect copy of a book to one so
MADE-UP.' Many collectors, faced with the choice in a
very early or a very rare book, would agree. But the
trouble is that even if such restoration—and it can be
astonishingly convincing—was 'honest and unconcealed'
in the first place, the passage of time and changes of ownership may well have obliterated any but indelible evidence
when a later collector comes to consider the copy to which
it has been applied. Only when a facsimile has been made
with intent to deceive (e.g. a first edition title for a second
edition) is the result a *fake* in the proper sense; but the
collector is concerned less with the motive than the fact.

When the whole volume, or a whole section, has
been WASHED, difference in the paper is the most likely
warning of a facsimile leaf or leaves; for washing and the
subsequent ironing will largely reduce, if they do not
remove, the most important difference between a page of
print and the same page reproduced by any photographic
or lithographic process—viz. that in the former the letters
are impressed into the paper, while in the latter they lie
upon it. This difference, in an unwashed leaf, can be seen
if it is tilted against the light, and felt by any reasonably
sensitive finger. Even good pen-facsimile, which at its
best is better than photography, is often betrayed under a
powerful glass by the fact that the edges of the letters tend
to be too smooth.

Yet these and all the many other tests will only avail, in
the case of a skilful facsimile, *once suspicion has been aroused.*
This is not to suggest that the collector should suspect a
facsimile at the sight of *any* washed, ironed or repaired leaf;
any leaf which differs slightly in size from its neighbours;
any leaf whose stains, OFFSET, WORMHOLES or other
peculiarities do not correspond with its neighbours'. He

may have before him nothing worse than a made-up copy.
But it is better to be over-sceptical than over-trusting when
a leaf or leaves in a book have a fishy look or feel.

It remains to add that facsimiles have been made—
never, presumably, with honest intent—of armorial,
Grolier, 'Canevari' and other prized types of leather
binding. Also of PUBLISHER'S CLOTH bindings, of which
three well-known examples are Galsworthy *Villa Rubein*
1897, Samuel Butler *The Way of All Flesh* 1903 and
Katherine Mansfield *Bliss* 1921.

FANFARE BINDINGS

'A style of bookbinding decoration developed in Paris in
the 16th century having the following characteristics: a
continuous interlaced ribbon, bounded by a double line on
one side and a single on the other, divides the whole surface
on both covers into symmetrical compartments of varying
shapes and sizes; the central compartment is the most
important and may be empty; the other compartments are
generally filled with gilt tooling, the ornament often including naturalistic leafy branches.' (A. R. A. Hobson)

The fanfare style was imitated, with varying degrees of
fidelity, all over Europe. Its name derives from a much-
admired pastiche executed by Thouvenin in 1829 for
Charles Nodier upon a copy of a book called *Fanfares et
Corvées abbadesques*.

FAVOURITE EDITION

A term applied by antiquarian booksellers to some edition,
never the first and not necessarily an early one, which has
at one time been ESTEEMED and may (or may not) be so
still. While seldom wilfully misused, it is often the re-
flection of a slightly out-of-date taste.

FILLET, FILLETED, FILLETING

The fillet is a binder's tool: a revolving wheel with one or
more raised bands on its circumference for impressing a
line or parallel lines on the leather or other binding material.

In the description of books the term is commonly used to mean the line or lines produced by the tool. It is seldom if ever used except of leather binding. Since about 1700 filleting has generally been gilded. A *French fillet* is a triple fillet, always in gold, the lines unevenly spaced.

FINE PAPER COPY

In the seventeenth century, when much printing paper was of rather poor quality, a small proportion of some books would be printed on a superior paper, often Dutch. Again, in the second half of the eighteenth and in the early nineteenth century part of an edition might be printed on a superior or thicker paper, at an advanced price; these were commonly advertised as on *fine paper*, but are sometimes described today as *thick paper* or *special paper* copies. (cf. LARGE, ROYAL, IMPERIAL paper).

FIRST EDITION

Very, *very* roughly speaking, this means the first appearance of the work in question, independently, between its own covers. But, like many other household words, this apparently simple term is not always as simple as it appears. The question *When is a first edition not a first edition?* is a favourite debating exercise among bibliographers and advanced collectors; and some contributions to the confusion will be found in the present work under the entries on EDITION AND IMPRESSION, ISSUE AND STATE 'FOLLOW THE FLAG', SERIALS, SECONDARY BINDINGS, AUTHORISED EDITION, PIRACY, PART-ISSUES, FIRST PUBLISHED EDITION, ADVANCE COPIES, COPYRIGHT EDITIONS, PRE-FIRST, BOOK FORM, FIRST SEPARATE EDITION.

FIRST ENGLISH EDITION

First edition published in England of a book which had previously been published abroad: e.g. Shelley's *Adonais* (Pisa 1821, Cambridge 1829), Macaulay's *Essays* (Philadelphia 1841, London 1843). Sometimes (but better not) used for the first translation into English of a book already published in another language.

See also 'FOLLOW THE FLAG'.

(1) This term is occasionally used by publishers (mostly in U.S.A.) in the statement of edition which in most modern books is placed on the back of the title-leaf; thus: 'First printing', 'First printing March 1920, Reprinted May 1920', 'First and second printings before publication'. In the same sense (=impression) it is used by bibliographers when stating, and thence quoted by booksellers when emphasising, the number of copies produced. Thus: 'The first printing was of 1,750 copies', 'This first printing was limited to 525 copies'.

See EDITION AND IMPRESSION.

(2) In a different sense it is used to mean the first appearance of any work in print, when this was in some other than separate form. *The Times* of 31 October 1917, for instance, would be catalogued as containing the 'first printing' of Housman's 'Epitaph on an Army of Mercenaries' (of which the 'first edition in BOOK FORM' was *Valour and Vision*, 1920, while it was 'first COLLECTED' in *Last Poems*, 1922). Or again, of Mrs. Hemans's *The League of the Alps*, etc., Boston, 1826, the cataloguer would say 'this edition contains the first printing of the author's best-known poem, *Casabianca*'.

FIRST PUBLISHED EDITION

This implies that the edition so described was preceded by another (or even more than one) printed for private, official or similarly restricted circulation and not offered for sale to the public.

FIRST SEPARATE EDITION

The first edition between its own covers of something previously published with other matter.

FLEURON

A printer's typographical ornament, originally flower-shaped.

FLOATED COPY

'This term refers to books which were once INLAID [2 (b)], then removed from the inlay and bound again, though now of course separate leaves. They may be recognised by a slight curl at the edges where the glue has left a permanent trace.' (W. A. Jackson.)

FLY-LEAF

Strictly speaking, this term means a binder's BLANK additional to, and following, the free front ENDPAPER. It is, however, often used of the free front endpaper itself.

FLY-SHEET

A single sheet printed on one or both sides, somewhat smaller in size than a BROADSIDE or broadsheet.

FLY-TITLE

A second HALF-TITLE is sometimes found, in 19th and 20th century books, placed between the last page of the PRELIMS and the opening page of text. This is called a fly-title. The term is also sometimes used of DIVISIONAL TITLES in abbreviated form.

FOLDED

Unsewn, unstitched; usually of leaflets and the like, if the implication is that the piece was so issued; but occasionally referring to some accidental failure to complete the process of book production; e.g. 'a remarkable copy, in the folded QUIRES as issued to subscribers'.

FOLIATED, FOLIATION

Foliation is the numbering of leaves, as opposed to PAGINATION, which is the numbering of pages. It is rare in books printed before 1475, when the majority bore no consecutive numeration at all; or after 1600, by which time it had generally given place to pagination.

FOLIO

(1) A leaf numbered on the RECTO, or front.
(2) The numeral itself in a FOLIATED book or MS.
(3) A book of folio size—see FORMAT.

'FOLLOW THE FLAG'

The name given to a controversy which raged during the 1930's, which still occasionally breaks out, and which must always survive among collectors of English and American first editions of the 19th and 20th centuries. The question at stake is whether the axiom that first means first is, or is not, to be modified when a book is first published (whether by arrangement, by accident or by PIRACY) elsewhere than in the author's own country.

With a few reluctant exceptions, French bibliographers ignore the claim of such editions on the attention of the collector: avoiding the dilemma of chronological priority by the use of the term *édition originale*, which means, not the first edition, but the first authorised edition published in France. English and American collectors have so far found no such convenient formula for reconciling logic with sentiment. And their problem remains a serious one; for if many of Rousseau's and Voltaire's and Balzac's books were first published outside France, a quite surprisingly large number of sought-after English and American books of the past hundred and fifty years were first published on the opposite side of the Atlantic from their authors.

It is these, rather than occasional earlier examples like More's *Utopia* (Louvain, 1516), which cause the trouble. Thanks to the more careful author-bibliographers, and in particular to the pioneer work of I. R. Brussel,[1] the facts are fairly well established for most of the authors who have been actively collected in the past. But the decision to prefer (and therefore to be ready to pay more for) the actual first or the native first rests with the individual collector. The keen author-collector will of course want both. The general, or the eclectic, collector may either adopt one rule or the other, or he may treat each case on its merits; perhaps giving some weight to an authorised over a piratical edition, probably giving more to the length of the interval between the first and the first native. The Philadelphia edition of Lamb *Last Essays of Elia* 1828, for example, preceded the London one by five years; but the New York edition of Stevenson *Dr. Jekyll and Mr. Hyde* 1886 had the advantage by no more than five days.

[1] *Anglo-American First Editions*, Bibliographia Series, no. IX, 1935, and no. X, 1936.

Special problems are presented by the work of authors who have long resided, or even become naturalised, on the other side of the Atlantic; e.g. Washington Irving, Henry James, T. S. Eliot, Aldous Huxley, W. H. Auden. With them, perhaps, chronological priority is the only alternative to chaos. But in the main field of debate the logicians have been losing ground steadily to the sentimentalists.

See also AUTHORISED EDITION, PIRACY.

FORE-EDGE PAINTING

This can refer to any painted decoration on the fore-edges of the leaves of a book, such as was not uncommon in the 15th and early 16th centuries, especially in Italy.

The term is most commonly used, however, for an English technique quite widely practised in the second half of the 17th century in London and Edinburgh, and popularised in the 18th by John Brindley and (in particular) EDWARDS OF HALIFAX, whereby the fore-edge of the book, very slightly fanned out and then held fast, is decorated with painted views or conversation pieces. The edges are then squared up and gilded in the ordinary way, so that the painting remains concealed (and protected) while the book is closed: fan out the edges and it reappears.

The technique was practised by a few other English binders of the late 18th and 19th centuries, and a certain number of undoubted examples survive. But it has been very briskly revived (in response to collectors' demand) in the present century: sometimes as an avowed modern craft, on modern books, but more often applied to suitable earlier books with intent to deceive. Some of these pastiches are remarkably skilful, so that it is often very difficult indeed to decide whether an individual fore-edge painting was executed in 1790 or 1970. Recognition of this fact, combined with the substantial output of bogus examples, has by no means blunted collecting enthusiasm. But it has made responsible booksellers, and should make all collectors, wary. (By way of an authentic revival, a series of fore-edge paintings, signed and dated, were executed by Miss C. B. Currie for Sotheran's of London between the two world wars.)

FOREL or FORREL

A term used rather loosely to denote inferior PARCHMENT, generally left in its natural colour—off-white or yellowish cream.

FORGERY

Forgery, which implies a deliberate fraudulent intention, is mainly confined, for our purpose, to autograph manuscripts, letters and documents, to inscriptions or annotations in books, and similar written, as opposed to printed, matter; and to fine early bindings. Though the word is properly applied to some printed examples of the art—the 1493 *Columbus Letter* and Thomas J. Wise's 19th century pamphlets, for instance—the openings for it are severely limited.

The faking of books by the insertion of facsimile leaves is discussed above, under FACSIMILES AND FAKES. See also MADE-UP.

FORMAT

This term (nowadays pronounced to rhyme with doormat) is defined by OED as 'the shape and size of a book'. In bibliographical contexts it is used to indicate the size of a volume in terms of the number of times the original printed SHEET has been folded to form its constituent leaves: modified when necessary by the subsequent make-up. Thus in a folio each sheet has been folded once, in a quarto twice, in an octavo three times; the size being thus respectively a half, a quarter and an eighth that of the original sheet. If the folded sheets have been gathered straightforwardly for sewing, then size and format will be indicated by a single term, e.g. quarto: if otherwise, the format of the completed volume will be expressed as, e.g. quarto in eights. (See GATHERING.) The methods of folding in books of the smaller sizes (especially 12mo and 24mo) have often varied and the bibliographical results are sufficiently complicated to drive most amateurs to MC-KERROW (pp. 164 and following). But though the sizes of sheets vary substantially, thus producing subdivisions in the size of books, a terminology based on the method of folding has been found satisfactory for all but eccentrically shaped volumes.

The principal formats, with their common abbreviations, are:

Folio (Fo., of late years sometimes 2°).
Quarto (Qto, 4to, 4°).
Octavo (Oct., 8vo, 8°).
Duodecimo (12mo, 12°, sometimes pronounced twelve-mo).
Sextodecimo (16mo, usually pronounced sixteenmo).
Vicesimo-quarto (24mo, pronounced twentyfourmo).
Tricesimo-secundo (32mo, pronounced thirtytwomo).

It is the technical terms of the paper trade which provide the names—such as pott and elephant (deriving from water-marks)—for the sub-categories of size. But most book-sellers' catalogues nowadays dispense with a terminology which is increasingly unfamiliar to, and unnecessarily technical for, the majority of their readers. These know—or should know—that, from the early 17th century at least, a folio is a large upright-shaped volume and an octavo a small upright-shaped volume, while a quarto (between them in size) is essentially squarish in shape. And where special precision is necessary—to distinguish between different ISSUES or variants, or to establish a LARGE PAPER COPY —this is commonly effected by giving the measurements of the leaf.

Large folio, small folio, large quarto, small quarto are terms in constant use. But even the four main subdivisions of format—(downwards) royal, demy, crown, foolscap—are in practice almost never used for anything but 4to and 8vo.

Foolscap is sometimes abbreviated to f'cap. Demy is accented as in defy.

To understand format, read MCKERROW: see also Graham Pollard's 'Notes on the Size of the Sheet' (*The Library*, Sept.–Dec., 1941).

FORME

The forme (or form) is the body of type, locked by the compositor into a frame called the *chase*, which makes up

whatever number of pages are to be printed at one operation of the press on one side of one sheet. By extension it
is used to mean the whole of the matter so printed, independent of its arrangement as subsequently folded.

FOUNT or FONT
(OF TYPE)

The style and size of the type. In the strict sense a printer
would order from the typefounder 'a fount (i.e. complete
set) of pica (= 12-point) Caslon'. But its commonest use,
in bibliographical contexts, is in such phrases as 'the first
issue, with the author's name in a different fount from the
title', or 'the earliest state of p. 163, with the two wrong
founts (i.e. alien types) in the word *peppercorn*'.

FOXED, FOXING

Of paper: discoloured, stained, usually with brownish-
yellow spots. E.g. 'EDGES foxed as usual', 'PLATES foxed',
'a fine copy except for some foxing'. Foxing is due to
chemical action in paper which has been badly bleached
in manufacture, usually caused by damp or lack of ventila-
tion. Some authorities derive the term (first noted in 1848)
from the colour of the spots: most are silent on its origin.

FRAME

When used in descriptions of binding, whether of leather
or (more often) cloth, this properly means a hollow
rectangular design, usually simple, running parallel to the
four edges of the cover, but with a space between it and
them. If they were ever all used on the same book, the
frame would be inside the BORDER but outside the PANEL.

FRONTISPIECE

An illustration facing the title-page of a book (or, occasionally, of a division or section of a book). In COLLATING
an illustrated book which has no list of illustrations but in
which, as often, the plates themselves are numbered in
sequence, it should be remembered that the frontispiece
is seldom included in such numeration.

FULL

(OF BINDING)

Full CALF or full MOROCCO simply means bound in calf or bound in morocco. The term is used, seldom necessarily and mostly just for emphasis, in contradistinction to HALF or QUARTER binding.

GALLEY PROOFS, or GALLEYS

Early PROOFS, pulled on long strips before the type has been locked up in the FORME. The galley is the printer's tray, and galley proofs usually contain the type for about three pages. Although recorded as early as 1773, they came into general use only in the 19th century. Inconvenient for reading, galley proofs pose an ugly problem in preservation and shelving. Yet even if they carry no marginal corrections by the author, they are prized by some collectors as containing the uncorrected state of the text (and the printer's errors and misprints).

GATHERINGS

A gathering (or quire or section) is the group of leaves formed after the printed sheet has been folded to the size of the book and before it is combined in proper order with its fellows for binding. The SHEET is the printer's unit, the LEAF the bibliographer's: the *gathering* is the binder's. In octavos the gathering normally comprises one sheet folded three times; but in larger or smaller volumes it may consist of two or more sheets (for folio or quarto books), or of half a sheet (for duodecimos and below). For sewing folios as single units wastes labour and thickens the spine of the binding, whereas 24mo or 32mo foldings sewn in one are apt to impose a strain on the thread and to lie uneasily in the finished book. A volume of which the gatherings consist each of four leaves is said to be 'in fours': it may be a folio in fours (i.e. one folio sheet sewn within another), a quarto in fours (i.e. sewn as folded), or an octavo in fours (i.e. gathered in half-sheets). In the 16th century folios were in fact commonly gathered 'in sixes' (i.e. three sheets per signature); in the 15th century normally in ten.

GATHERINGS (continued)

Each gathering usually has a SIGNATURE in the lower margin of at least the first leaf, for the binder's guidance in assembly. (*See, for instance, p.* 97.) The centre of the gathering in the completed book can be identified by the thread with which it has been sewn. (*See, for instance, between pages* 104 *and* 105.)

See also COLLATION, FORMAT, HALF-SHEETS, INSERT.

It is nowadays common to find gatherings referred to as *signatures*—e.g. 'wormholes in the last two signatures' or 'complete with the blank leaf, which is part of the signature'.

GAUFFRED (or gauffered, or goffered) EDGES

Gilt (or silvered) edges decorated by the impression of heated tools, usually of the POINTILLÉ type.

GENERAL TITLE

If several parts of a book are sufficiently different from one another to justify DIVISIONAL TITLE-PAGES, the omnibus title-page at the beginning is known as a *general title*. Similarly, if several works published independently are later collected for RE-ISSUE as a composite volume, they will usually be provided with a general title. This is likely to be dated (if at all) with a later year than any of the original title-pages.

GESAMTKATALOG DER WIEGENDRUCKE
Leipzig, 1925, etc.

Commonly abbreviated to Gesamtkatalog or GKW or GW, this exhaustive catalogue of 15th century printed books reached, with the first fascicle of its 8th volume (1940), the letter F. Edited by a committee of German INCUNABULISTS, with much expert assistance from all over the world, it will presumably be, if ever completed, the definitive work in its field. The text is in German. The arrangement is alphabetical by authors. Location of all known copies of an edition is given when the recorded total is less than ten.

GIFT BINDING

This term is used (*a*) generally, of any leather binding done for presentation—school prizes, Christmas presents, etc. —not from the author; and (*b*) in a special sense, of certain types of PUBLISHER'S BINDING designed, in wholesale quantity though often only for part of the edition, for the gift market. These are sometimes described as *presentation bindings*: a less convenient term, from its liability to confusion with an AUTHOR'S BINDING.

GILT EDGES

Unless specially qualified (e.g. GILT TOPS), this means that all three edges of the book have been cut smooth and gilded.

GILT ON THE ROUGH

A technique common in French but rare in English binderies, by which the edges of the leaves are gilded without being first cut smooth. It is designed to give the collector the best of both worlds—the elegance of gold without any sacrifice of margin; but it does not, like smooth gilt edges, keep the dust out.

GILT TOPS or TOP EDGES GILT

Interchangeable terms meaning that the top edges only have been gilded, and implying that the other edges have been cut smooth or at least trimmed. If they have not, the book is described as *gilt tops, other edges uncut* or simply *t.e.g., uncut*. Some binders deplore the plural for either.

GOFF

Incunabula in American libraries. A Third Census, compiled and edited by Frederick R. Goff. New York, The Bibliographical Society of America, 1964.

First published in 1919, and long familiarly known as Stillwell (Miss Margaret Bingham Stillwell having edited its successor in 1940), this census now runs to 47,188 entries. Its finding-list formula is fully buttressed with references to BMC, HAIN, GKW, etc., and besides being constantly cited by cataloguers it is thus found increasingly useful, being alphabetically arranged by author, as a first reference book for INCUNABULA.

Outside specialist literature this is the accepted general term (though see below), and on the whole the most satisfactory one, for all those many varieties of type which look 𝖗𝖔𝖚𝖌𝖍𝖑𝖞 𝖑𝖎𝖐𝖊 𝖙𝖍𝖎𝖘, as distinct from roman (the kind of type in which this book is printed) or italic (the kind of type in which this *word* is printed).

There are three main groups of such types. The first is the *textura* or 'pointed text' letter of the Gutenberg Bible, most early liturgical printing and the first edition (1611) of the King James Bible. (This variety is still sometimes called *black letter*, especially, and with some fitness, for English books.) The second is *rotunda*, which was common in Italian printing until well into the 16th century, and longer in Spain. The third is *bastarda* (Caxton's first type is an example), of which one form, *fraktur*, had the longest life of them all.

Gothic types were the earliest ever designed, for the German pioneers naturally followed the manuscript bookhands prevailing north of the Alps in the middle years of the 15th century. Although in Italy these types lost ground fast to the roman letter, regional variations of Gothic were almost universal in the printing houses of France, the Low Countries and England, as well as Germany, till well after 1500. Outside the German-speaking and Scandinavian countries, however, roman and italic gradually relegated gothic type to liturgical and legal printing and cheap vernacular books, to which, with a few exceptions (such as newspaper titling, funerary matter, and Yuletide greetings), and certain archaistic or nationalistic revivals, it has mostly been confined in recent centuries.

GRANGERISED

See EXTRA-ILLUSTRATED

GROLIER LIST

The Grolier Club of New York (called after Jean Grolier, a French bibliophile of the 16th century renowned for the beauty of the bindings executed for his books) has published many valuable exhibition catalogues and other bibliographical reference books. One of these is commonly cited without amplification, viz. *One Hundred Books Famous in English Literature* (1902); thus an American collector will say that he possesses 78 of 'the Grolier Hundred', or a cataloguer will headline a book as 'on the Grolier List'. (See HIGH-SPOTS)

GUARDED

A guarded leaf or PLATE is one which is pasted, by its inner edge, on to a prepared STUB, instead of being CONJUGATE with another and thus sewn in as part of the GATHERING. For illustrations, which are often printed separately from the text on single leaves and need special care, guarding has been a common practice in book-production since early days; and the fact that they are so set in a book will not require mention in a catalogue description.

But guarding is also a method of repair for old books which have given way in the folds, for leaves or plates which have come loose and got frayed at the inner edge, or for others which have been weakened by damp; e.g. 'title and frontispiece guarded', or 'last few leaves guarded'. If such leaves have actually been restored at the inner edge, they would be called EXTENDED; if at the outer edge, RE-MARGINED.

See also CANCELS, TIPPED IN.

GUIDE LETTERS

d
Uring the early decades of printing the manuscript practice persisted, though dwindlingly, of leaving initial letters to be put in by the hand of the ILLUMINATOR or RUBRISHER. Since some of these craftsmen were no great scholars and therefore might not be sure what letter the word should begin with, the initial letter would sometimes be printed, very small, in the space left for painting. When the initials were put in, care would be taken to paint over these *guide letters*, as they are called; but when, as not infrequently happened, the book never was rubricated, the guide letter remains, rather forlornly, in the middle of an empty square.

GUTTA-PERCHA, or CAOUTCHOUC, BINDING

An invention of the versatile Thomas Hancock, this process, by which a rubber solution takes the place of sewing for holding the leaves together, has been employed at intervals by bookbinders since about 1840. Lear *Nonsense Rhymes* 1846 was an early example, and the process was used for many of the illustrated 'table books' of the 1860's. In most 19th century books so bound the rubber has perished, so that some, if not most, of the leaves have come loose. Since they are cut flush at the back, instead of being GATHERED in QUIRES as for normal CASING, it is difficult to make a tidy job of RE-SETTING them.

HAIN

Repertorium Bibliographicum, etc., by Ludwig Hain, 2 vols., 1826–38, and recent photographic reprints.

An alphabetical list, by author (and where author unknown by title), of 16,311 books printed before 1501: about 45% of the total now recorded. Hain marked with an asterisk descriptions made from copies he himself had examined.

Although seriously out of date in technique, and far from comprehensive, Hain is still cited in descriptions of INCUNABULA; and deservedly for its fullness and accuracy where (but only where) he had examined the book.

A *Supplement* by W. A. Copinger was published in 3 vols., 1895–1902. This is usually cited as *Hain-Copinger*. K. Burger published *Indices* to Hain in 1891 and D. Reichling a series of *Appendices* beginning in 1905.

HALF BOUND

This normally means that the spine and outer corners are of leather (or VELLUM) while the rest of the sides are covered with cloth or paper (often MARBLED). Catalogue descriptions usually specify the kind of leather, and *half morocco* or *half calf* will be seen twenty times for every use of *half bound*; which indeed (except in the sparsest type of descriptive formula—where it will probably be abbreviated to *hf.bd.*) is seldom used unless the leather concerned is of some low-grade type, like roan or sheep, which it would be discouraging to specify.

Half calf, reputed an English invention, goes back to the 17th century but only took firm hold in the early 18th. Half morocco is rare before 1800.

If there are no leather corners, the book is said to be QUARTER BOUND; if the leather corners are very wide, it is said (rarely nowadays) to be THREE-QUARTER bound. *Half bound* may also be used of a volume put up (not EDITION-BOUND) in cloth back and paper sides.

HALF CLOTH, QUARTER CLOTH

Cloth spine, usually with the title printed on a paper label, and paper board sides (no corners). A common publisher's binding style from the late 1820's for about fifteen years, found regularly on three-volume novels as late as the early 1850's, and occasionally on books of any kind since about 1890.

Also used at any date since 1830 by jobbing binders, and in this context sometimes (and more correctly, on the analogy of HALF BOUND *v*. QUARTER BOUND) known as *quarter cloth*.

HALF-SHEETS

The technicalities involved in *printing* on half-sheets (strictly imposition by half-sheets) are a matter of concern only to graduate bibliographers, who know more about it than I do; and others are referred to MCKERROW, p. 66, where it is fully described.

The average collector meets the term in its other sense, viz. *gathered* in half-sheets, quite frequently at the beginning of the COLLATION or description of books printed before 1800. For we often find those of the smaller sizes (16mo, 24mo and 32mo) to be sewn in gatherings of half the number of leaves in the sheet, viz. 8, 12 and 16 respectively. In the 18th century 8vos were sometimes made up in the same way. This modification of the regular method of gathering is expressed by some bibliographers as *16mo in eights*, by others as *16mo in half-sheets*.

See FORMAT, GATHERING.

HALF-TITLE

The leaf in front of the title-page (and of the FRONTIS-PIECE, if any) which carries on its RECTO the title (sometimes abbreviated) of the book, possibly a volume number or indication that the book belongs to a series, rarely the author's name, and very occasionally the price. The VERSO is often blank, but sometimes carries the printer's IMPRINT, or in modern books (*like this one*) a list of other works by the same author or from the same publisher.

(N.B. Sir Walter Greg, for 17th century books, used the term half-title to cover also FLY-TITLES and even what I have called DIVISIONAL TITLES. Printers sometimes, and the Bibliographical Society of America, use the old fashioned term *bastard title*. Some American bibliographers call half-titles fly-titles and *vice versa*, which is maddening.)

The use of a preliminary BLANK LEAF, to protect the title-page from dirt and damage before binding, was not uncommon in earlier days; but the addition to this leaf of some identification of the book dates from the second half of the 17th century. The half-title, as this leaf came to be called, has since become a common, though never universal, feature of book production.

Half-titles can be a great nuisance to collectors (and booksellers). Binders of the past removed them more often than not: partly as being inessential, like blank leaves; but in earlier days also from that ulterior motive which made binders so ruthless with margins—an eye to their sack of waste paper, which, sold back to the mills, provided a source of subsidiary revenue. It is not always easy to tell whether a book without a half-title should have one or not, unless there is a published COLLATION to refer to. Normally the half-title will be the first leaf of the first GATHERING in the book, so that if examination shows that this unit is short of a leaf at the beginning, the inference is that the copy lacks either a half-title or a preliminary blank. Even so, only comparison with other copies will show which it was. But since PRELIMS are usually printed last, and since their make-up is by their nature often irregular, an apparently even collation of the first gathering does not always mean that the book had no half-title; for this may have been printed on a final blank or other spare leaf, to be severed for binding in its proper place.

HALKETT AND LAING

Dictionary of Anonymous and Pseudonymous English Literature, by Samuel Halkett and John Laing, 4 vols., 1882–88. New and enlarged edition by James Kennedy, W. A. Smith and A. F. Johnson, 7 vols., 1926; vol. 8, covering the years 1900–1950, and vol. 9, Supplementary, by Dennis Rhodes and Anna E. C. Simoni, 1956, 1962.

Arranged alphabetically by the first word of the title, with an index of authors. Halkett and Laing is not exhaustive and its attributions are not all equally authoritative; but it is the best thing of its kind.

It is less often mentioned by cataloguers than would be expected, seeing what a large number of books were published anonymously or pseudonymously. This is because its attributions are regarded as common property and are not normally credited to their source. Consequently, it is most commonly cited in such references as 'not in Halkett and Laing', or 'attributed by Halkett and Laing to Bacon, but actually written by Shakespeare'.

HAND-LIST

Defined by SOED as 'a list of books, etc., in a form handy for reference', this term is commonly applied today to something considerably fuller than a SHORT-TITLE list or a librarian's 'finding list', but considerably less full than a descriptive bibliography (cf. CHECK-LIST).

HARD-GRAIN MOROCCO

A kind of goatskin used for binding, which when dressed has a very close, even, pebbly texture; the grain or pattern being much tighter than in LEVANT, the leather itself firmer and, when made up, harder than NIGER. It cannot be so highly polished as levant.

HARLEIAN STYLE

A description (often incorrectly applied) of an 18th century style of binding. It derives from the name of Robert Harley, Earl of Oxford (*d.* 1724), and of his son Edward; great collectors, to both of whom Humfrey Wanley was librarian, and for both of whom the majority of their important bindings were executed in the 1720s by Thomas Elliott and Christopher Chapman. The general characteristics of the authentic Harleian style are: (1) an elaborate, if sometimes rather narrow, BORDER, made up of one or more ROLLS; (2) a large central ornament, usually in the shape of an elongated lozenge, built up from a number of small units; (3) the predominant bright red colour of the MOROCCO leather, specially imported from that country (see also TURKEY).

HAYWARD

English Poetry, A Descriptive Catalogue; First and Early Editions of Works of the English Poets from Chaucer to the Present Day. National Book League, 1947. (Illustrated edition, with corrections, 1950).

This catalogue of John Hayward's personal but authoritative exhibition, with its valuable annotation, has over the years come to be cited by booksellers and auctioneers' cataloguers simply as *Hayward*; partly because it describes a number of books by authors who have to date no bibliography of their own, partly because it has achieved the distinction of a sort of Parnassus. (cf. GROLIER LIST)

HEADBAND

A decorative band, usually of silk or cotton, plain or coloured, worked over leather, cord, rolled paper, or (occasionally) cane, and fastened inside the top and sometimes also the bottom of the back (or spine) of a book as part of the process of binding. These headbands are sewn in to the leaves and sometimes also to the boards. Since the introduction of the kettle-stitch into western binderies headbands have been technically unnecessary; but though functionless for the past 200 years they have persisted as a decorative accessory, especially in recent years, to give a CASED book the air of having been truly bound.

Binders use headbands in the plural to mean head- and tailbands.

HEADLINE

'A line of type at the top of a page, above the text, is called a headline; or, if it consists of the title of the book (or of the section of the book) on every page or every opening (i.e. two pages facing one another), sometimes a "running-title" or "running-head"' (MCKERROW).

The Cambridge University Press's Manual, *Preparation of Manuscripts and Correction of Proofs*, distinguishes usefully between *page heads*, for book-title, section-title or chapter-title, and *running heads* for those headlines, usually on the right-hand page and changing with each turn-over, which indicate the contents of the two pages under view.

HEAD-PIECE

A type-ornament or VIGNETTE at the head of a chapter or division of the book.

HIGH-SPOTS

'High-spot' collecting is a sort of dictated eclecticism. Somebody or other has listed or selected one particular book by an author as his best, or the commentator's favourite, or simply the one thought to be the most esteemed by collectors. And in due course people who collect on the *table d'hôte* rather than the *à la carte* system concentrate on this particular work to the exclusion of all the others, thus condemning themselves to blinkers and frustration and their booksellers to despair. Less prevalent than of yore.

HINGES

It would be convenient if *hinge* were always used to denote the inside junctions and *joint* the outside junctions of the sides of the binding with the spine. In practice, however, they are used almost indiscriminately, as are the terms *re-hinged* and RE-JOINTED for books which have been reinforced or repaired at these vulnerable points. There is, certainly, a tendency towards the suggested distinction: 'hinges weak' is more likely to refer to the inside, and 'JOINTS weak' almost certainly means the outside. But the

HINGES (continued)

binder's term *morocco joints* refers to the inside, and there is enough room for confusion in current usage to make some clear ruling desirable.

HISTORIATED

Of initials, capitals or borders, in manuscripts or early books: properly meaning decorated with *histoires*, i.e. figures of men or animals, rather than with floral or formal designs.

HOLLOW BACKS

'A form of binding in which the cords are recessed but the leather back [SPINE] is not glued or pasted on to them, so that when the book lies open the sides and the back all rest flat on the table, but the recessed cords bend upwards leaving a semicircular space between them and the leather back' (Graham Pollard).

This technique was devised in France, in the second half of the 18th century, to make flat-back-bound books (see FRENCH-SEWN) lie open. Adopted in England *c.* 1820.

HOLOGRAPH

Adjective (not noun): meaning entirely in the handwriting of the author. It is commonly used of literary manuscripts as distinct from AUTOGRAPH letters, annotations, inscriptions, etc.

HORÆ, or BOOKS OF HOURS

Manuscript or printed collections of prayers, etc., for private devotional use at the canonical offices of the Roman Church. Variations of detail between one diocese and another are indicated by such phrases as 'Horæ of the Use of Rouen', or 'a Book of Hours of the Sarum Use'.

The output of manuscript Horæ, during the 14th and 15th centuries particularly, must have been immense. The majority of printed examples derive from the years between 1490 and 1520, with Paris as the most active centre of production.

114

HORN-BOOK

'A leaf of paper containing the alphabet (often, also, the ten digits, some elements of spelling, and the Lord's Prayer) protected by a thin plate of translucent horn, and mounted on a tablet of wood with a handle' (SOED). Horn-books were used from the 16th to early 18th centuries to teach children their rudiments, and A. W. Pollard once stated[1] that authentic examples were rarer than First Folio Shakespeares, since they were the kind of thing nobody at the time troubled to preserve. This may have been true in 1911: it may, for all I know, still be true to-day of authentic early horn-books. But for every genuine original there are probably a dozen modern fakes—some clumsy, some skilful—prompted by the high price of originals and the fact that no two are identical.

IDEAL COPY

This term, increasingly popular among American bibliographers, is applied only to books before about 1800, in which corrections were customarily made during the course of printing. Though it is possible for an individual example of the book in question to conform to it, the 'ideal copy' is a sort of Platonic archetype, exhibiting the final intention of the author, publisher and printer at the completion of printing, in so far as this is capable of being established. The ideal copy takes no account of changes or corrections demonstrably introduced after publication. But it is equally, and more significantly, distinct from that earliest state of the text—more often displaying errors or survivals of incomplete revision than considered intention— the pursuit of which has become habitual to many collectors.

See ISSUES AND STATES.

ILLUMINATED, ILLUMINATION

This general term means decorated by hand, whether in formal, floral or HISTORIATED style, in gold and/or silver and/or coloured paint. It is used of initial letters, single words, first lines or opening pages of (usually very early)

[1] *Encyclopædia Britannica,* 1911, article 'Book Collecting'.

printed books; but much more often of manuscripts, the margins of which may be extensively illuminated and which may contain full-page MINIATURES.

ILLUSTRATION PROCESSES

These are of two kinds: (1) the more or less direct product of an artist's tool and (2) photographic.

The photographic reproduction processes are line-block, half-tone, photogravure, collotype, etc.

The other group, which includes most illustrations of interest to collectors of older books, may be divided into three sub-groups: (*a*) relief printing—e.g. WOOD-EN-GRAVING, WOOD-CUTTING; (*b*) intaglio—e.g. copper and steel ENGRAVING, drypoint, mezzotint, etching, aquatint; (*c*) planographic—e.g. lithography.

For technical details the reader is referred to *Processes of Graphic Reproduction in Printing* by Harold Curwen; for an historical introduction, to A. M. Hind *A History of Engraving* or Singer and Strang *Etching, Engraving and the Other Methods of Printing Pictures*, which contains a full bibliography.

See also COLOUR-PLATE BOOKS.

IMPENSIS

Latin for *at the expense of*: used in IMPRINTS or COLO-PHONS of early books to identify the publisher or financially responsible bookseller or patron.

IMPERFECT

Used only of the interior of a printed book or manuscript; imperfections or damage to the binding being usually indicated by such terms as DEFECTIVE. An imperfect copy, anathema to fastidious collectors, is seldom so called unless it is pretty seriously incomplete; absent BLANKS, HALF-TITLES, ERRATA slips, etc., being generally just noted as 'lacking'.

IMPERIAL PAPER COPY

Imperial, like *royal* or *crown* (see FORMAT), is the paper-maker's name for a particular (large) sized sheet. But the term *imperial paper copy* was used loosely—and perhaps grandiosely—in the 18th and early 19th centuries as a synonym for LARGE or FINE PAPER COPY.

IMPRESSION

(1) The number of copies of an edition printed at one time (see EDITION AND IMPRESSION); e.g. 'the first impression was of 500 copies only', or 'later impressions of the first edition bore no date on the title-page'.

(2) The term is also used of the quality of a piece of printing or (on a binding) stamping; e.g. 'with fine impressions of the plates', or 'only early copies such as the present one have a really sharp impression of the engraved title', or 'with unusually clear impressions of the arms (*see* ARMORIAL) on both covers'.

IMPRIMATUR

Latin for *let it be printed*: the formula, signed by an official licenser of the Press (whether secular or religious), authorising the printing of a book. Hence, by transference, an official licence to print. Such licences, common in 16th and 17th century books of all countries, are usually printed at the beginning of the book; sometimes on a separate leaf, hence *licence leaf*.

Cf. PRIVILEGE.

IMPRINT

A notification to the reader (and to the legal authorities) of the person or persons responsible for the production of a book. Some of the earliest printed books bore no such note; but from about 1465 till late in the 16th century the *printer's imprint* was generally placed at the end of the book (and there properly called the COLOPHON). It normally comprised the place of printing, the name of the printer and the date.

With the development of the title-page during the 16th century the printer's imprint tended to be transferred thither (even if it was repeated at the end of the book); and from the latter half of the 16th to the end of the 18th century it was often combined with the *publisher's imprint*, in such forms as *Printed by A.B. for P.Q.* or *for P.Q. and R.S.* (sometimes with the further notice *and are to be sold by Y.Z.*). Later, the lower half of the title-page came generally to be reserved for the publisher's imprint—again normally comprising place, name and date; the printer's name (and perhaps address) being relegated either to the back of the title (*as in this book*) or of the half-title, or to the end of the volume; in the 18th century it was frequently omitted altogether. Either kind of imprint may be accompanied by the printer's or publisher's DEVICE or mark. From 1799 the law (39 George III cap. 79) required the name and abode of the printer to be given on anything he printed. This regulation is still, I am told, on the statute book, but it must have been broken many thousand times by now.

Imprint is also used for the publisher's name stamped on the spine of the binding (or printed on a paper label).

INCUNABLE, INCUNABULA, INCUNABULIST

The special use of *incunábula* (Latin for 'things in the cradle') to mean books produced in the infancy of printing has for many years been further specialised to mean books printed before 1501. The Englishing of the word, in singular as well as plural form, as *incúnable(s)* is nearly a century old (the old-fashioned term was *fifteeners*). For some of the most frequently cited reference books see BRITISH MUSEUM CATALOGUE, PROCTOR (arranged geographically by printers); GESAMTKATALOG DER WIEGEN-DRUCKE, HAIN, GOFF (alphabetically by authors).

Its original, wider use for 'the earliest stages in the development of anything' (OED) has been revived in such phrases as (of the May 1839 Bradshaw) 'one of the incunabula of Railroadiana', or (of Einstein's early papers) 'the incunabula of the theory of relativity'.

INDIA PAPER

(1) A confusing abbreviation for *India Proof Paper*, which is identical with CHINA PAPER, used for proofs of engravings; hence, *India paper proofs* or *India proofs*.

(2) *Oxford India Paper:* a very thin, tough, opaque printing paper first successfully made in 1875 for the Oxford University Press in imitation of oriental papers.

INLAID

(1) Of bindings: the use of coloured leather or leathers inserted into spaces cut in the main skin, to produce a MOSAIC effect. Cf. ONLAID.

(2) Of paper: (*a*) the insertion of a leaf or a PLATE or a CUT in a larger and usually stouter leaf, to enlarge its margins, and thus its whole size (often in order to range with other, larger leaves in a composite volume, when it is usually described as *inlaid to size*); (*b*) the laying down, or re-margining on all four edges, of a badly damaged leaf.

INSCRIBED COPY

Unless specifically qualified, this term means that the copy has been autographed or inscribed *by the author*. It often implies, further, that the copy has been inscribed *to* somebody or *for* somebody, or that a sentiment of some kind accompanies the signature.

It is important to distinguish between a PRESENTATION COPY, which is a spontaneous gift, and a copy inscribed by the author, often some while after publication, in response to an owner's request. The former naturally appeals much more strongly to the sentiment of collectors. The distinction is not, of course, always possible, since an author may genuinely present a book years after its publication date, or again may phrase an inscription written to oblige a stranger in the same terms as he would have used for a friend. And booksellers would not be human if they did not give ambiguous cases the benefit of the doubt. More often than not, however, the circumstances can be inferred from the wording of the inscription and the relation of its date (if any) to that on the title-page.

INSCRIPTIONS

Unlike INSCRIBED, the term *inscription* carries of itself no implication that the author of the book is responsible. Inscriptions (on endpaper, fly-leaf, title-page, etc.) unconnected with the author or anyone else worth specifying will usually be mentioned in a bookseller's catalogue only if they are on the one hand prominent or extensive enough to be something of a defacement, or on the other hand seem of some intrinsic interest; though an important or expensive book will of course be more fully described in this as in other particulars.

Modern books, however, are sometimes described as 'with inscription on endpaper, otherwise fine' even when the original owner has merely written in his name and perhaps the date. This rather finicky attitude, adopted in deference to the mint-condition fetishists, is resented by collectors who have a respect for a book's PROVENANCE, particularly at an early stage.

INSERT, INSERTED, INSET

It is convenient to treat these terms together. An *inset* is defined by SOED as 'a folded section of paper placed within another, completing the sequence of pagination; an extra page or set of pages inserted in a sheet or book; an advertisement on a separate leaf inserted in a magazine, etc.' An inset or inserted leaf or leaves may be integral to the book as printed and gathered for binding; e.g. 'complete with the leaf of preface, which is an insert (or inset)', 'with the inserted plan at p. 148', etc. Inserted ADVERTISEMENTS, by contrast, are normally printed independently of the books for which they are intended and are variable in their incidence in different copies. Finally, there is matter inserted in a book by one of its owners which, though usually associated in some way with it, is both structurally and by original intention entirely distinct; e.g. 'portrait inserted' (this implies that the portrait does not belong in the book), 'two leaves inserted from a shorter copy' (i.e. MADE-UP), 'autograph letter from the author inserted' or the like.

When used in this last sense, *inserted* generally means

bound in, sewn in or stuck in. When letters, cuttings or other such things are not physically attached to the book, they are properly described as *laid in* or *loosely inserted*.

INTEGRAL

A leaf is said to be integral, or sometimes integral to the COLLATION, when it is part of the GATHERING: as distinct from a single leaf INSET in a gathering though printed independently of it; and even further distinct from some leaf like a binder's BLANK or inserted ADVERTISEMENT. E.g. 'lacking Q8 which, although it carries only the printer's imprint, is integral to the collation', or 'complete with the blank leaf R4, integral to the last SIGNATURE (or gathering) but usually missing'.

INTERLEAVED

When a book is bound with blank leaves alternating with the printed leaves it is said to be interleaved.

INTERNATIONAL LEAGUE
OF ANTIQUARIAN BOOKSELLERS

Founded in 1948, ILAB or LILA (Ligue Internationale de la Librairie Ancienne) is a confraternity of the principal national associations, with an internationally elected president and committee, which provides certain common services to, and exacts certain common services from, its member-associations. The League publishes an international directory of member-booksellers and an international glossary (eight languages) of book-collecting terms. Otherwise, until it produces its long-meditated code of ethics for antiquarian booksellers, or unless his own delinquency in paying his bills qualifies him for inclusion in its international black-list, ILAB's impact on the average collector will probably be limited to his recognition of its device on some booksellers' catalogues.

ISSUES AND STATES

When alterations, corrections, additions or excisions are effected in a book during the process of manufacture, so that copies exhibiting variations go on sale on publication day indiscriminately, these variant copies are conveniently classified as belonging to different *states* of the edition. (An exception is the regular use of *issue* for variant title-pages, usually in respect of the publisher's IMPRINT.) It may or may not be possible to determine priority of manufacture between them, but any priority of PUBLICATION must be assumed to be accidental. When similar variations can be clearly shown to have originated in some action taken after the book was published, two (or more) *issues* are distinguishable.

It is, of course, perfectly possible for different issues and different states to co-exist within an edition. For instance, some corrections may have been made to the text during printing (producing variant *states* of the leaves involved). Then one fearful howler, pilloried by a reviewer, has to be dealt with by substituting a corrected leaf (or CANCEL) in the copies still undistributed, which will thereafter constitute a *second issue*. Yet copies both of the first and second issue are likely to show an indiscriminate mixture of variations of state, none of which (it must be repeated) has any bearing on the question of priority of issue.

Since differences of issue are bibliographically tidier and more straightforward than differences of state, and since the term falls much more pleasingly on the priority-conscious ear, a good many undeterminable cases have been, and no doubt will continue to be, given the benefit of the doubt. Yet in fact the onus of proof that an observed variation derives from a deliberate action taken *after* publication lies, or should lie, like an iron weight on the conscience of anyone who begins to write the word *issue*. It is a salutary, if rather too sweeping, proposition that all variants of this kind should be called *states* until they have been proved otherwise—or simply left as VARIANTS.

See also EDITION AND IMPRESSION, THE CHRONO-LOGICAL OBSESSION, POINT-MANIACS, MISPRINTS, CANCELS, SECONDARY BINDINGS.

ISSUE-MONGERS

The issue-monger is one of the worst pests of the collecting world, and the more dangerous because many humble and well-intentioned collectors think him a hero to whom they should be grateful. He may be a bibliographer (usually the self-styled type), or a bookseller, or a collector, and his power for harm may be rated in that order. He is an honours graduate of what Lathrop Harper called 'the fly-spot school of bibliography'. He is the man who, if he cannot construct a bogus POINT out of some minute variation he himself has discovered between two copies of a book, will pervert the observations of others to the same purpose. Show him a MISPRINT or a DROPPED NUMERAL, and he will whip you up an 'issue-point' in no time. Show him a difference of a month between two sets of inserted publisher's catalogues and he will be good for a whole paragraph of dubious inferences. Show him a wrappered PROOF COPY of a book which he happens not to have seen in that state before, and his cry of 'TRIAL ISSUE' or 'PRE-FIRST edition' will turn Pollard or McKerrow in the grave.

His natural and unlamented prey are the POINT-MANIACS. But unfortunately his more numerous victims are those collectors credulous enough to accept anything they see in print or hear declaimed with sufficient assurance.

It is fair to say that issue-mongers are today (1971) not as numerous, as confident, or as influential as they were 20 years ago when the preceding salvo was fired; which suggests that collectors and booksellers are more sensible than they were in my youth.

JANSENIST STYLE, JANSENISTE

(OF BINDING)

Originally a French style of the late 17th and early 18th centuries, in which outside covers of austere plainness were usually combined with an elaborate DOUBLURE or inside cover. As standardised by more modern binders, the outside is generally absolutely plain, while in England at least the doublure has largely given place to regular endpapering with DENTELLE decoration or a deep border of multiple FILLETING in gilt.

JAP(ANESE) VELLUM, JAPON

Kinds of paper, rather stiff, with a very smooth glossy surface (not unlike VELLUM, hence the name), usually pale yellowish buff in colour; mostly used for ÉDITIONS DE LUXE. *Japanese vellum* (in French, *papier de japon*) is a costly paper, hand-made in Japan. *Japon* (*anglice*) is a British-made imitation.

JOINTS

The use of joints for the exterior, HINGES for the interior, junctions of the spine of a volume with its sides is to be encouraged, as a convenient distinction. Joints seldom need to be mentioned in the description of a copy unless there is something wrong with them; and the degree of their shortcoming is likely to be indicated in the order *rubbed, tender, weak, cracked, loose, defective, gone*.

See also RE-JOINTED.

JUVENILES

Children's books. A jargon word, but well established; borrowed from the publishing trade. To be distinguished from *juvenilia*, a writer's youthful productions.

KEY BOOKS

A key book is to a subject what a HIGH-SPOT is to an author: supposedly the most important (or earliest significant) work in its field. It is a term very liable to ignorant or pretentious misuse, and it is fortunately less popular than it once was.

LABEL

(1) *Leather* labels (or lettering-pieces) on the SPINE have been used by binders since the late 17th century. Generally of a different colour from that of the main skin, and almost always of MOROCCO pared very thin (even if the book itself is bound, or HALF-BOUND, in CALF), they display, usually in gold, the title of the book, the volume number (if necessary), the name of the author (sporadically before the late 18th century, regularly since), and since 1800 sometimes also the date. When two labels are used, some-

times of different colours, the conventional description is 'double lettering-pieces'.

(2) *Paper* labels, printed from type or occasionally engraved, began to be used in the second half of the 18th century on the paper spines of BOARDED books (the earliest known examples date from the 1760's). They must have been almost universal during the first quarter of the 19th on books put up in this form; and they continued as the regular method of titling for boarded books even after this style was generally displaced by PUBLISHER'S CLOTH. They were also used on the early cloth books, though with sharply decreasing frequency after 1832, when the process for applying titling and decoration directly on to the cloth was perfected. And they were standard on HALF CLOTH. At least since 1800 they seem usually to have been printed along with the book; often, no doubt (indeed certainly in some cases, where they have accidentally survived undisturbed), on a spare blank leaf, or on a leaf which would otherwise have been used for a half-title.

The printed paper title-label has never died out. It was revived extensively in the 1890's and again in the 1920's, though with a slightly precious air. Publishers have in modern times recognised its friability and tendency to get dirty by the provision of a spare label, TIPPED IN at the end of the volume. And if the collector notices that the paper label on a copy of, say, Max Beerbohm *Works* 1896 or Strachey *Queen Victoria* 1921 is surprisingly fresher than the adjacent cloth, he will probably find that the spare has been put to its intended use.

(3) *Library* labels: see EX-LIBRARY.

(4) See LONGITUDINAL LABELS.

LAID DOWN
See MOUNTED (2)

LAID LINES
See WIRE LINES

LAID PAPER
Paper made, originally in a frame or mould, on a mesh of close-set, but distinguishable, parallel wires crossed at right

angles by other wires set at a considerably wider, but variable, interval. The marks of these wires, visible in the finished paper when held up to the light, are called WIRE (or *laid*) LINES and CHAIN LINES respectively. (WOVE paper is made on a mesh of wires woven together, and in its natural form shows no such marks.) Before about 1800 all paper, both laid and wove, was made by hand; some superior papers continued to be, and still are. Inevitably, paper-makers soon learned to impart to machine-made paper, manufactured on a continuous travelling wire web, the superficial characteristics of laid paper. In modern papers, therefore, it is not possible to distinguish hand-made from machine-made papers by the presence of chain-lines or even of a WATERMARK, since these may be present in a superior (or a pretentious) machine-made paper.

LARGE PAPER COPY

One of a (usually small) number of copies printed on a larger size of paper than the main bulk of the edition; either for presentation, or for subscribers, or to be sold at a higher price. The paper will often be of superior quality; and, in the 18th century particularly, these were generally called *fine* or *royal* or *imperial* paper copies. (Copies of 17th and early 18th century books with unusually wide margins are sometimes optimistically described as being on large paper without any real justification.) Extravagantly large paper makes an unsightly book, unless the type is reset to accord with the increased page-size; for the result is all too often a blob of type in an expanse of margin.

In default of positive evidence, it is safer to assume that large paper copies will have been *printed* after, rather than before, the main part of the edition, though they will very likely have been *published* simultaneously.

LAW CALF

Smooth CALF of a rather disagreeable yellowish fawn colour still used for binding (or, more usually, HALF

BINDING) law books. It should not be confused with ROUGH calf, which in the past was used for law books as well as several other classes.

LEAF
The basic bibliographical unit: the piece of paper comprising one page on its front side (recto, obverse) and another on its back (verso, reverse). Leaf, leaves are abbreviated to l., ll., or f., ff. (from FOLIO). The inaccurate and slovenly misuse of *page* for *leaf* (e.g. 'the verso of p. 73,' 'the title-page is a cancel') appears to be on the increase and should be pilloried when found.

LEAFLET
SOED defines this as 'a small-sized leaf of paper, or a sheet folded into leaves but not stitched, and containing printed matter, chiefly for gratuitous distribution'.
    Cf. BROADSIDE, FLY-SHEET, PAMPHLET.

LEATHER
When this is used without the kind of leather (e.g. CALF, MOROCCO) being specified, it is usually of something so undistinguished as to be not worth (commercially) identifying, such as SHEEP or ROAN. Or its nature may even have baffled the cataloguer.

LETTERED DIRECT
This means that the title, author's name, etc., have been stamped straight on to the binding material, whether leather, cloth or paper boards, instead of on to a LABEL or LETTERING-PIECE, as has been the general practice since about 1700.

LETTERING-PIECE
A synonym for LABEL when made of leather.

LETTRE BATARDE
See GOTHIC

LEVANT

A kind of loose-grained MOROCCO leather, considered during the past hundred years the most elegant of the family. It is usually highly polished. As its name implies, it came originally from the Near East. More recently the best has been produced in French North Africa and usually dressed in France. Today most of the levant skins made up in English binderies come from South Africa and are known in the trade as 'Cape levant' or 'Cape goat'.

LIBRARY BINDINGS

In collectors' parlance this always refers to circulating, not to public or institutional, libraries.

The circulating libraries used from their earliest days (they were founded in the 1720's) to commission their own binding, generally of half leather, often with uncut edges. This practice seems to have been maintained until PUBLISHER'S CLOTH became the standard uniform for fiction. The results, however, are seldom positively identifiable, unless betrayed by library labels (see EX-LIBRARY).

In the second half of the 19th century special cloth bindings executed, in wholesale quantity, to a library's order may have been less infrequent than we know; but very few certain examples have been recorded. George Eliot *Felix Holt* 1866 is one. The regular practice of the circulating libraries was to buy their books in the publisher's cloth, as they still do.

Practically all 20th century books in library bindings have been *re*-bound from their original cloth, and their edges probably cut down in the process. No collector will touch a copy in such a library re-binding with a ten-foot pole unless he has given up hope of anything better.

LIBRARY EDITION

An edition, or a collective set, printed in a large-sized readable type; suitable for the library of a gentleman.

LICENCE, LICENCE LEAF
See IMPRIMATUR

LIMITATION NOTICE

The printed (or, rarely, hand-written) certificate stating how many copies of an edition of a book, or of a particular part of an edition, have been printed; often, but not invariably, followed by the serial number of the individual copy. E.g. 'Of this LARGE PAPER edition (*or* this edition on hand-made paper, *or* this signed edition) *x* copies have been printed. This is No. *y*'. If there is more than one special impression, the details of each may be rehearsed; e.g. 'Of this edition *a* copies have been printed on VELLUM, *b* copies on hand-made paper, signed by the author, and *c* copies on JAPANESE VELLUM, of which this is No. *d*'.

The French have, since the 18th century, carried this sort of thing much farther than we have; and the *justification du tirage* in a modern French book designed for the bibliophile market will often occupy half a page.

See also LIMITED EDITION, ÉDITION DE LUXE, LARGE PAPER COPY, OUT OF SERIES.

LIMITED EDITION

Any edition which is limited to a stated number of copies (books described as limited editions which fail to specify how many copies they are limited to should be regarded with scepticism). But see also OUT OF SERIES.

The motives for such limitation are several. (*a*) If there are illustrations, the number of satisfactory impressions to be got from the plate or block or stone may determine the size of the edition; (*b*) if the book is printed by hand, the pressman's enthusiasm for first-class work is apt to decrease after a certain point; (*c*) the publisher considers that the book will sell better if a scarcity value is created from the start; (*d*) the publisher estimates that the potential sale of the book is *x* hundred (or thousand) copies, and decides, when printing so many and no more, to make a virtue of necessity by adding a formal limitation notice.

However small the number of copies of a limited edition, collectors will do well to remember that the magic of a limitation notice is sufficient to ensure that fewer of them than of an ordinary book will have been thrown away or sent for salvage or roughly used; and that the more ignorant the owner the more potent the magic. Consequently, an edition 'limited to 1,750 copies each signed by the author' is likely to be much less rare today than an ordinary edition of the same number of copies—or fewer—which was not ostentatiously limited. And while an edition limited to a small number (100 or less) has an initial claim to rarity which time cannot positively reduce, the passage of years will do less than usual to enhance it.

LIMP

This term is used of binding not based on board sides. Limp vellum was common in the 16th and 17th centuries, and was revived by private presses at the end of the 19th. Limp cloth was, and occasionally still is, used as a publisher's binding for slim, cheap or educational works. Limp leather was commonly used for road-books, etc., in the last quarter of the 18th century and the first quarter of the 19th; but for the past hundred years it has been more or less restricted to devotional books and sentimental verse, sometimes finished with YAPP EDGES.

LININGS or LINERS

A synonym for the binder's endleaves when these are of some special material, such as VELLUM or watered silk. When they are of paper, they are called ENDPAPERS; when the PASTE-DOWN (as opposed to the free half) is of leather it is called a DOUBLURE.

LIST PRICE

The original published price of a book: sometimes printed (usually in brackets) alongside the catalogued price of a second-hand copy or a REMAINDER as a demonstration that the prospective buyer is getting a bargain. Worldly-wise collectors are apt to react in the opposite direction, assuming, not always correctly, that if something is quoted below par, it cannot be worth buying. (Audubon's *Birds of America* could be had for half-price in the 1850's, and several of Shelley's first editions were remaindered.)

LONGITUDINAL LABELS

Title-labels, printed vertically up the leaf in large type, which are quite often found still in place (i.e. not detached for use) in certain English books between 1650 and 1700. Their purpose, though the subject of much learned debate, has not yet been certainly determined. They are a great nuisance to collectors of the books for which they were provided, since they were customarily printed on an INTEGRAL leaf (usually of the first or last GATHERING), and it is therefore a moot point whether a copy is or is not complete without them. The majority would say incomplete, on the analogy of HALF-TITLES or BLANK leaves, which were often discarded by the binder. But since, whatever their exact purpose, these longitudinal labels were almost certainly intended to be cut out before the volume was completed by binding, their survival unused belies the printer's and publisher's intention. They are truly analogous, therefore, with those leaves of the first or last gathering in three- or four-volume books of the boards-and-label period, on which were printed the set of labels to be divided and pasted on to the spines. The fact that these, unlike the longitudinal labels of the 17th century, very rarely survive unused is neither here nor there: the point is that no one would consider such books incomplete without them.

LOOSE

Used mostly of books in PUBLISHER'S CLOTH and meaning that the book has been so badly shaken that its continued connexion with its covers is precarious. Such a copy is described as *loose in covers* or *binding loose* or simply *loose*.

In descriptions of books bound or half bound in leather, or books in boards, *front cover loose* or *back cover loose* or even *covers loose* will probably mean that one or other or both are actually detached.

LOWNDES

The Bibliographer's Manual of English Literature, by William Thomas Lowndes, 4 vols., 1834. Revised by Henry G. Bohn, 1858–64 (several times reprinted).

Lowndes is out of date by modern standards of completeness and precision. But it is a most useful reference book, and it contains a great deal of information for the collector which is not easily found elsewhere.

'LYONNAISE' OR 'LYONESE' BINDINGS

Commonly but misleadingly used of two styles developed in the later 16th century often found on small volumes *printed* in Lyons but not so far demonstrably bound there (rather than Paris): (*a*) with broad geometrical strap-work designs painted, lacquered, or enamelled; (*b*) with a large centre ornament (roughly lozenge-shaped) and large corner ornaments in gilt, the ground generally covered with dots or small ornaments.

MADE-UP, MADE-UP COPY

A made-up copy is one whose imperfections—the lack of a single leaf or more—have been made good from another copy of the same edition. The term is seldom met with in booksellers' catalogues, since making-up is often either unrecognised or unavowed. But a scrupulous cataloguer describing such a copy, especially of a book so rare or important that shortcomings may be pardoned, will specify it as having, e.g. 'pages 63–66 from another and shorter (*or* equally clean) copy'.

Making-up with leaves from a copy of a different (usually later) edition—i.e. faking-up—is a bibliographical felony and valid grounds for divorce between buyer and seller.

MAGAZINE PRINTING

SEE PERIODICAL PRINTING, SERIALS, BOOK FORM

MAJUSCULE, MINUSCULE

Majuscules are what printers call *upper-case* and ordinary men capital letters. Minuscules are the *lower-case* or small letters. *Even caps*. means THIS. *Caps. and small caps*. or *smalls* means THIS. *Even smalls* means THIS. *Caps. and l.c.* (for lower-case) means This.

MANUSCRIPT

Written by hand. With ILLUMINATED OR CALLIGRAPHIC

manuscripts the criterion is antiquity or beauty, or interest of script or decoration. With literary manuscripts, authenticity and/or interest of content. Collectors of the latter ought not to need reminding that *manuscript* or *manuscript additions*, *notes* or *corrections* will not be in the author's handwriting unless they are also described as AUTOGRAPH or HOLOGRAPH.

MARBLED

Marbled paper is made by lowering a sheet of paper on to a bath of gum or SIZE, on the surface of which colours have been drawn out with a stick or comb into a pattern. It is found in Japan as early as 1118 (called Sumingagashi), but the Persians seem to have been the first to use marbled paper for books. Imported from the Levant, it was in use in Holland before 1600, but it was not manufactured in western Europe till 30 years later. Its use for END-PAPERS had spread from France to England by the 1650's, and it was the commonest material for covering the sides of HALF BOUND or QUARTER BOUND books of the 18th and 19th centuries.

Marbled morocco was used in Paris in the mid-16th century, and in England about a century later, along with *marbled calf*. *Marbled edges* are executed by a modification of the same technique as is used for marbling paper. Used from about 1780 till the 1830's for books bound in RUSSIA or half russia and commonly since on books in CALF or half calf (MOROCCO-bound books have always, normally, been given gilt edges). *Marbled cloth* had a brief vogue with publishers in the 1850's, and has been occasionally revived since.

MARGINS

'The white margins of a page are called the head, tail, outer and inner margins, the inner being of course that nearest to the fold of the paper (or the back of the book)' —MCKERROW. The inner margins of a page-opening are sometimes called (but not by printers) the gutter, and the tail is generally called the lower margin.

☛ *This is the inner margin, this is the outer margin* ☚

See CONDITION, DECKLE EDGES, UNCUT.

McKERROW

An Introduction to Bibliography for Literary Students, by
Ronald B. McKerrow. Oxford, at the Clarendon Press,
1927. Second Impression with corrections, 1928.

McKerrow is to bibliography what Erskine May is to
parliamentary practice—the indispensable basic manual in
matters of fact, the classic authority in matters of judgment.
Subsequent research and discussion have produced modifications in detail (see, for instance, Professor Fredson
Bowers' *Principles of Bibliographical Description*, 1949)
and McKerrow's doctrines are certainly less than final for
modern books. But bibliographers disagree with him at
their peril on questions of principle.

MINIATURE

(1) To *miniate* (from *minium*, meaning red lead) meant
originally to colour or paint with vermilion, to RUBRI-
CATE or ILLUMINATE. But *miniatures* have come to
denote the painted scenes, anecdotes, groups of figures or
the like, distinct from conventional decoration and by
implication more ambitious than HISTORIATED, with
which the professional artists of the monastic *scriptoria*
or secular *ateliers* decorated medieval and renaissance
manuscripts (and occasionally some special copy of an
early printed book). Such pictures would often be full-
page; and since the page would not necessarily be of small
size, the term *miniature*, subject as it is to pseudo-etymo-
logical confusion, is not a very happy one. But it is no
doubt too late to change it.

(2) Miniature books: the accepted term for books whose
principal (usually only) interest lies in their very small
size. Any volume below $2'' \times 1\frac{1}{2}''$ would probably qualify.

MINT CONDITION

A term borrowed from the numismatists, meaning as good
as new, and extended to such uses as 'mint copy', 'dust-
jacket defective, otherwise mint'. Not to be encouraged.

MISBOUND

When a leaf or leaves, or an entire GATHERING, has been
wrongly folded or misplaced by the binder, it is called

misbound. Provided that nothing is missing, and that the amount of matter misbound is not too great or its misplacing too glaring, collectors commonly take a more charitable view of the result than readers.

MISPRINTS

'There is a very important difference', says MCKERROW, 'between errors of wording and errors of printing (which alone are properly called "misprints").' Yet misprimped words or page-numerals are probably the most frequently cited of any of those features in a book which may, or may be alleged to, bear upon its priority of issue over another copy of the same edition. E.g. 'first issue, with the misplanted numeral on p. 113'; 'first issue, with all the mosprints uncorrected'.

This sort of note has an exciting, a reassuring, sometimes an almost mesmeric effect upon collectors whose respect for bibliographical minutiæ is insufficiently salted with scepticism; and it is, of course, irresistible to the POINT-MANIACS. These latter will be temperamentally averse from the recognition, which cannot be too strongly impressed upon the former, that the existence of a midprint or milprints in one or several copies of a book is not, in itself, any evidence of priority of issue over another which has the same word or words correctly printed.

In the days of the hand-press, indeed, corrections were commonly made in the type after some sheets had already been printed off; and misplints were often so corrected. Yet the sheets will have been gathered for folding and binding without regard for priority of printing, so that corrected and uncorrected sheets will be combined indiscriminately in the finished copies of the book as handed across the counter on publication day. (See ISSUES AND STATES.) Thus, even if there is clear evidence of the correction of an originally mimprinted word, the most that can normally be said of a copy that shows it uncorrected is that it has the earlier state of that particular leaf; and no more. There is usually, moreover, nothing (unless the PROOF sheets have survived) to prove that the word was not correctly printed in the first place; the musprint being caused by some loose types falling out during the run and being incorrectly replaced. (See also DROPPED LETTERS.)

There are, of course, cases in which it is clear, from the provision of an ERRATA slip or leaf, that mispronts were observed after a certain number of complete copies had been printed off. And if other copies are found to have these corrections made in the text, there is a *prima facie* case for classifying them as a definitely later consignment; though it is seldom possible to establish whether they constitute a later state (i.e. corrected before publication), a later issue (i.e. incorporating changes made after some copies were actually on the market), or even a distinct, but undifferentiated, second IMPRESSION (the whole book having been put to press again).

During the past century, when the hand-press had given way to the machine for ordinary book-work, misfrints will seldom have been corrected at the press, nor will they very often have been dealt with by the troublesome method of CANCELLING the offending leaf and substituting another. They are usually left alone, if they are not too obtrusive; and if they must be corrected, the quarter-sheet, the half-sheet, or even the whole SHEET will be reprinted. It follows that many minor misprilts in modern books, which are from time to time joyfully hailed as proving that a copy containing them is of 'the rare first issue', persisted throughout the entire first edition (if not through later ones), so that such copies are elevated at the expense of a 'second issue' which never existed.

As part of the evidence from which a bibliographical conclusion can be drawn, or a probability established, or a hypothesis constructed, masprints, like any variation between one copy of the same edition and another, have their usefulness. But as the sole and unsupported foundation for a claim to priority they are the merest reeds.

MITRE, MITRED

A binder's term with several meanings. In the workshop it is used for any lines which meet at right angles without crossing; and also for a junction of lines at an angle of 45 degrees, such as is necessary at the leather turn-in on the inside of the covers.

By writers on binding, and thence by cataloguers, the term is also used to denote the connexion at the angles of an outer FRAME to an inner frame or PANEL by the diagonal use of FILLETS or a ROLL.

MODERN FIRSTS

A category widely employed but (like EARLY PRINTED) impossible to define with any precision, since its use among antiquarian booksellers is, and probably always will be, quite unstandardised. At present (1971) it commonly extends as far back as 1900, and will perhaps include books published before that date if their author's heyday was after it. Yet I dare say that collectors in their teens or twenties would deny inclusion to any writer who was published before the First (or even Second) World War.

MOROCCO

A handsome, hard-wearing leather made of goat-skin and apt for dyeing in strong colours. Islamic in origin, the morocco leathers were first imported into western Europe through Turkey and Venice, domesticated in Italy early in the 16th century, north of the Alps early and in England late in the 17th. *Turkey* was the normal name in England in the 17th and early 18th centuries.

Today, *morocco* has no more geographical significance than its subspecies *levant* and *turkey*, for most of it used for binding comes from other parts of the world; and the only common denominator among the numerous varieties of leather which go under the name is that they are all goat-skin.

Of the various types of morocco commonly specified in catalogue descriptions, LEVANT, HARD-GRAIN and NIGER refer to differences of grain, pattern or texture in the actual skin when tanned and dyed; STRAIGHT-GRAIN and CRUSHED morocco refer to its treatment before it is put on the book; and morocco *extra*, *super-extra* or *elegant* (an old-fashioned term) refer to the degree of elaboration and the amount of gilt which have been lavished on it by the 'finisher' in the bindery.

MOSAIC BINDINGS
Leather bindings decorated with contrasting colours, whether INLAID, ONLAID or painted.

MOTTLED CALF
CALF which has been given a mottled effect, whether bold or delicate, by staining the leather with blots or flecks of acid (usually copperas).

MOUNTED
(1) Of engravings or other illustrations pasted down on to or lightly attached to a leaf, whether of ordinary text paper or some specially strong paper (e.g. cartridge).
(2) Of damaged leaves which have been laid down on or backed with paper (occasionally, for manuscripts, maps, plans or plates, with gauze or linen).

NEAT
This adjective, commonly used with special reference to the binding, strikes a rather submissive note. It means that the copy is decent, tidy and sound, but it suggests sobriety rather than elegance.

NEEDLEWORK BINDINGS
See EMBROIDERED BINDINGS

NIGER
A kind of MOROCCO (goat-skin). True niger, which comes from West Africa, is a soft skin with an unemphatic, variable grain. It is locally tanned and dyed (hence *native-dyed*); the favourite colours, seldom quite even, being crimson, orange to brick-red, green, or the natural buff. The slight variations of grain and colour which give niger its character are seldom successfully achieved in the imitations of it.

NO DATE
(N.D.)
This term, unqualified, means that research has failed (or has not attempted) to establish even an approximate date

for the book described. If the book itself bears no date but can be dated by external evidence, this is expressed either by 'n.d., but 1710', or 'n.d. [but 1710]', or simply '[1710]'.

NO PLACE, NO PRINTER, NO PUBLISHER

(INDISCRIMINATELY OR COLLECTIVELY SHORTENED TO N.P.) As for NO DATE. In descriptions of early books these terms will sometimes be found in their Latin forms—*sine anno, sine loco, sine nomine (s.a., s.l., s.n.)*.

NOT SUBJECT TO RETURN

When an auctioneer adds to the description of an ordinary book the words *sold not subject to return*, or the initials *w.a.f.* (with all faults), it is because he fears or suspects that it is imperfect and therefore suspends his normal guarantee that the book offered is at least all there.

Certain classes of books are, by convention, sold not subject to return without any such implication. Among these are: (1) fine bindings, as being prized for their covers rather than their contents; (2) ASSOCIATION books, whose value, again, is largely independent of their completeness; (3) atlases and books or sets of doubtful composition (including some COLOUR-PLATE BOOKS); (4) magazines and periodicals; and (5) collections of pamphlets or tracts—such things, in fact, as it may be either impossible or unreasonably laborious to COLLATE accurately. Books issued in PARTS also are sometimes (and for good reason) sold 'not subject to return for the absence of INSERTED ADVERTISEMENTS'.

For manuscript material the principal auction houses of London and New York, while offering no guarantee of completeness, nowadays accept the return within a specified period of anything which the buyer can establish to their satisfaction to be a forgery.

OASIS

A proprietary name given to a goat-skin imported from Nigeria, tanned and dyed in England, popular with contem-

porary binders. The skins have a rather smooth surface
but are sometimes attractively grained. (Kenneth Hobson.)

OCTAVO

The commonest size of book since the early 17th century.
A large (demy) octavo is about the size of a biography or
travel book; a small (crown) octavo about the size of an
average modern novel.

For details see FORMAT.

OFFPRINT

A separate printing of a section of a larger publication
(generally of composite authorship) made from the same
setting of type. Offprints are occasionally given their own
pagination, often have a paper wrapper or some similar
individual covering, and sometimes have a special title-
page. They are prized by collectors of their author far
above the composite publication (whether periodical or
book) from which they derive, for they are spiritually, if
not technically, a FIRST SEPARATE EDITION; they are
unencumbered with (to him) alien matter; and they often
bear a presentation inscription, since the normal purpose of
offprints is to provide the author with copies to give away.
The interchange of offprints between scholars working in
the same field has, indeed, become a regular method of
correspondence.

Where periodicals, sets of transactions and the like are
concerned, it is important to distinguish offprints from
EXTRACTS, for the one was intended to be an entity and the
other has been converted into one at a later date.

OFFSET

The accidental transfer of ink from a printed page or illustration to an adjacent page. This may be caused either
from the sheets having been folded, or the book bound,
before the ink was properly dry, or from the book being
subsequently exposed to damp. Offset from engraved or

other plates on to text, and from text on to plates, is commoner, and also much more disfiguring, than offset from text on to text.

Text offset occasionally provides valuable bibliographical evidence, since it usually derives from the very earliest stage in the assembly of the printed sheets into a book. And some of the neatest deductions have been made from the offset, not from one page to another of an individual copy, but from the offset on a page of one book from printed sheets belonging to another which happened to be stacked with it at the printer's. (The use of the word *offset* meaning a modern method of photographic reproduction is not likely to occur in booksellers' catalogues; but the collector should perhaps be aware of it.)

ON APPROVAL

Most booksellers will send a volume *on approval* on the assumption that the decision whether to keep it or not will not be unreasonably delayed. It has to be remembered, however, by anyone ordering a book on approval from a catalogue, that, unless he is an old or specially valued customer, preference is likely to be given to any firm order over any approval order. Some booksellers indeed (and not unreasonably) make a rule that they will not send a catalogued book on approval until a certain time after the catalogue has been in circulation.

ONLAID, ONLAYS

Used in the description of bindings, normally of leather, in which varicoloured decoration has been effected by sticking thin pieces of other leathers on to the main skin, thus giving a sort of MOSAIC effect. Cf. INLAID. The pieces are called *onlays*.

The technique was occasionally adapted to PUBLISH-ER'S CLOTH between 1840 and 1860, when the onlays were sometimes of paper.

ONLY

A note of warning, usually placed in parentheses. When, for example, a book is described as having '27 plates (only)' or a set as comprising '7 vols. (only),' it means that the series is incomplete.

ORIGINAL STATE or ORIGINAL CONDITION

As used—and very widely used—by cataloguers and collectors, this almost always refers to the book's exterior; and it will be found applied to books in cloth, boards, wrappers, leather or indeed any other covering for which the quality of originality can be claimed.

That it is claimed more often, especially of leather-bound books, than can in fact be substantiated, is an index of the steadily increasing importance attached to it since the last quarter of the 19th century; and indeed it is accepted doctrine with most collectors today that to a copy in a fine binding or an appropriate binding must always be preferred (other things being equal) a copy in original binding.

But how, asks the docile beginner, am I to recognise the original binding when I see it? He may well ask. The gradation of desirability between a Continental book in its original wrappers (*broché*), another copy in contemporary binding, and a third re-bound with its wrappers preserved, is outside the range of the present work. But for English and American books it is only of those produced after the date when publishers assumed responsibility for EDITION BINDING (say 1825–35) that it is possible to say with certainty that a particular copy is or is not in the original binding as issued. PUBLISHER'S CLOTH, notwithstanding the ugly question of SECONDARY and REMAINDER bindings, is to all intents and purposes a uniform, and collectors of Victorian or modern books have little difficulty in identifying it. The same is true of books (verse, pamphlets, PART-ISSUES, etc.) which were issued during the same period—indeed earlier—in an equally distinctive uniform of printed WRAPPERS or printed BOARDS.

It is when we get back past 1800 (to skate over the controversial period of the Regency) that the trouble starts: the 350 years during which the customer bought his book either unbound (though during the last decades probably in plain wrappers or perhaps lightly boarded) for binding to his own taste, or in some usually workaday binding put on it by the bookseller. In the former instance the book was still an embryo; and its covering, if any, though original, was intended to be ephemeral. In the latter, the binding will indeed be 'original binding as issued'; but since it was piece-work and not necessarily identical with its neighbours, how, after two or three hundred years, can it be distinguished either from a plain binding put on to a customer's order immediately on publication, or from one put on twenty or thirty years later? The answer is, not easily, and seldom with absolute certainty.

The much-debated question of *taste* between (a) wrappered or boarded books of the 18th century with wholly uncut edges, and (b) copies in original or contemporary leather with cut edges, is touched upon under CONDITION, DECKLE-FETISHISM, BOARDS, and elsewhere in the present work. The question of 'original leather' is discussed under TRADE BINDING.

OUT OF PRINT

This means that the publisher's stock of the book is exhausted (if temporarily only, the phrase is *out of stock*); and it implies that only second-hand copies are available. In antiquarian booksellers' catalogues it is naturally used only of recent books.

OUT OF SERIES

Of an edition specifically limited in number, there will usually be printed some extra copies or *overs*: (a) as a reserve against the possibility of spoiled sheets, misbinding or other technical hazards; (b) for the author, printer and publisher; (c) for review. Such copies are understood not to invalidate the certificate of limitation; and their status is sometimes indicated by the words *out of series*, instead of a number.

In numbered, limited editions which are also signed by the author, the out-of-series copies will not normally be signed. And unless they were the author's 'complimentaries' and were inscribed by him, they are rated by most collectors as slightly inferior to the regularly numbered copies.

PAGINATION

The sequence of figures with which the pages of a book are numbered. These are known individually as *page-numerals*, collectively as *pagination*. E.g. 'page-numerals shaved', or 'with the misprinted numeral on page 167'; 'first issue, with the irregular pagination in vol. 2'; or 'pagination in roman numerals'.

See also FOLIATION.

PALLET

A binder's term for a tool used to decorate the panels on the spine of a bound book. A specialised kind—properly called a *name-pallet*—can be used for lettering a whole word, name or title in one operation, as opposed to building it up by the impression of a series of single-letter tools. (William Hall, the binder, records that in the 1780's only one of the 'finishers' in John Bell's bindery was able to letter a book with single lettering, 'Mr. Bell having had the names of all his own publications cut in pallets—*Shakespeare, Theatre, Poets*, etc.')

The term is also used, of bindings since about 1800, for the impression of the binder's name on a SIGNED BINDING, when this is stamped inside the covers; sometimes accompanied by the name of the person or firm who commissioned the binding—e.g. 'Bound by Bagguley, Newcastle-under-Lyme', 'Doves Bindery 1902' or 'Bound by Birdsall for Charles Scribner's Sons'. Thus, when instructions are given to a binder, it may be stipulated that the book shall or shall not be palleted. The practice adopted by some booksellers of suppressing the binder's name in this context and having the volume palleted *Bound by* (instead of *for*) *S*— or *H*— or *B*— is to be deprecated, as likely to make unnecessary trouble for the Nixons and Hobsons of the future.

PAMPHLET

SOED defines this as 'a small treatise occupying fewer pages than would make a book, composed and issued as a separate work; always unbound, with or without paper covers'.

PANEL, PANELLED

A term used in the description of bindings, meaning a rectangle, formed of single, double or triple FILLETS (ruled lines), whether gilt or blind (plain), either on the sides or between the bands on the spine of the book. E.g. 'contemporary panelled calf'—and when used without qualification the word always refers to the sides; 'panelled MOROCCO, fully gilt back'; 'half LEVANT, panelled backs'; or, of a book in PUBLISHER'S CLOTH, 'in the earliest binding, with the panel on the front cover in gilt'.

Cf. FRAME, BORDER.

PANEL-STAMPED

Panel-stamps are 'large metal blocks, cut or engraved with a pictorial design, usually stamped on the book cover by means of a press' (J. P. Harthan). In use in the 15th and 16th centuries.

PAPER

See LAID, WOVE, CHINA, INDIA, JAPON, MARBLED, LARGE, ROYAL, IMPERIAL, THICK, CHAIN LINES, WIRE LINES, WATERMARK.

The most comprehensive reference book is *Dictionary and Encyclopaedia of Paper and Paper-Making* by E. J. Labarre (second edition, 1952, Supplement, 1969).

PAPER BOARDS

Technically, *paste-boards* are made from layers of paper, and *pulp-boards* (millboard, strawboard) from pulp. As commonly used in booksellers' catalogues, however, and notwithstanding that 'original boards' (see BOARDS (2)) are in fact covered with paper, the term *paper boards*, if used of any but quite modern books without qualification (such as original, marbled, flowered, decorated, Dutch), suggests boards of either species covered with paper of a plain colour, usually not the original binding.

PARCHMENT

The inner portion of the split skin (the 'under-split') of a sheep, not tanned but specially de-greased and dressed like vellum, either for writing on or for use in binding.

See also VELLUM, FOREL.

The practice of publishing books in instalments dates from the last quarter of the 17th century, when such a book—usually a work of popular instruction or inspiration, or a reprint—would be advertised as 'now issuing in numbers'. Publication in numbers or parts was common in the later 18th century for expensive illustrated books; and practically every one of the famous aquatint books of the early 19th was originally so issued. Encyclopædias (e.g. the first edition of the *Britannica*, 1768–71), dictionaries and similar substantial works of reference continued to be published in parts until the quite recent invasion of this publishing field by the instalment system. The amount of miscellaneous publication in this form during the 19th century—from *Moxon's Poets* and Newman *Apologia* 1864, Mrs. Beeton *Book of Household Management* 1859–61 and Gustave Doré's illustrated books, to the innumerable cheap adventure stories (or 'bloods')—was enormously greater than is generally appreciated.

But to most collectors *parts* means first and foremost the best-selling fiction published in this style from *Pickwick*, which started the vogue in 1836–37, to *Daniel Deronda* (1874–76), which was a late example. During this period most novels continued to be published in three volumes and *borrowed* by their readers from the circulating libraries. But a number of books by popular writers were published (usually with illustrations by a popular artist) in paper-covered parts, to be *bought* in instalments—monthly, fortnightly or weekly—and bound up when complete, sometimes in one, sometimes in two or more volumes, either in binding-cases supplied by the publisher, or in leather or half-leather to the owner's taste. These part-issues, which varied with the length of the book from 8 or 10 to 20 or 24 (and occasionally more) were mostly of large octavo size and usually sold for a shilling. The final part, which contained the title-page and PRELIMS, would often be a double number, when the complete set is described as 'in the original 13/12 parts'.

This method of publication was suited only to works

which might be expected to appeal to a large public. Among the Victorian novelists many of whose books were so issued were Dickens, Thackeray, Ainsworth, Lever, Surtees and Trollope.

Apart from any variations in the text or illustrations—and the often hurried conditions of printing for fixed publication dates produced a great many—part-issues present the collector with further complications all their own. The two chief ones concern (*a*) the wrappers, (*b*) the inserted advertisements. For fiction part-issues the *wrappers* were usually of coloured paper (Dickens in blue-green, Surtees in brick-red, Thackeray in yellow) with some pictorial or decorative design on the front, and advertising matter printed on the back, and more often than not on the inside of both front and back wrappers as well. The number of the part and sometimes its month of issue would be printed on the front wrapper. These last features naturally, and the three pages of advertisements frequently, changed with each issue; and since the replacing of damaged wrappers—theoretically from another copy of the same part but in practice often from another part—has always been a common and accepted form of MAKING-UP, the punctilious collector needs to assure himself that each part in any series has the right wrappers. It is not usually difficult to detect a changed part-numeral which would betray a wrong front-wrapper; but unless a detailed bibliographical description is available for reference, it is always difficult and sometimes impossible to tell on internal evidence whether the back-wrapper is correct or not. And as most surviving sets of parts have had their backstrips repaired, alien back-wrappers are not uncommon.

The question of *inserted advertisements*, both in general and with particular reference to part-issues, has been discussed under ADVERTISEMENTS.

It remains only to observe that whereas miscellaneous works, e.g. Herbert Spencer *First Principles* 1862, and penny dreadfuls, e.g. *Maria Marten, or The Murder in the Red Barn* 1828, are today very rarely found in their original parts, the Victorian novels so issued are mostly not nearly as uncommon as might be supposed from their fragile character and intentionally impermanent coverings. But it is true that they have very seldom survived in the fine unrestored condition which many collectors prefer to the most conscientious completeness of their sometimes highly touted advertising matter.

PART-ISSUED BOOKS IN VOLUME FORM

These are of little or no interest to the collector of part-issues as such, but their relationship to the parts is of interest, and sometimes of importance, to others. In the matter of priority, it was customary during the Victorian period for the complete volume, in the publisher's cloth, to be issued just before the publication of the final part, so that it ranks strictly as the first *published* form of the book. On the other hand, this publisher's volume-issue would generally be made up from the last-*printed* sheets of text and plates; so that although issued before any set of parts could have been completed, it would be apt to exhibit the latest state of any particular variant.

A further complication is provided by those copies of a part-issued book which, having been faithfully purchased in instalments, were sent to be bound up in the cloth case provided (at a stated price) by the publisher, or in the leather or half-leather styles which were also sometimes offered. Such a copy might well be of the earliest state as to text and plates; it would be in PUBLISHER'S CLOTH; yet as a completed entity (even if the local binder had not, as often, trimmed—or even SPRINKLED—the edges of the leaves) it is at some disadvantage *vis-à-vis* either a set of parts or the publisher's volume-issue.

It is usually possible to distinguish these cased-up sets of parts from the volume-issue (even when—as not always with Dickens, for example—the publisher's cases were uniform) by the presence in the former of the original STAB-HOLES. But when the distinction is made, it yet remains for bibliographers and collectors to assess the difference.

PASTE ACTION

The staining of ENDPAPERS, sometimes extending to the first or last leaves of the book itself, by the paste used for attaching the endpapers to the boards.

PASTE-DOWN

The paste-down is that half of the ENDPAPER which lines the inside of the cover (its other half is often called the *free endpaper*). Binders generally refer to the paste-down as the *board-paper*.

See also DOUBLURE, LINING.

PERFECT

(1) in the phrase 'collated and perfect'; (2) to perfect a sheet is the technical term for printing its second side; in a bibliophilic context one may refer to perfecting an imperfect copy; (3) a type of thermoplastic binding often used for paperbacks (see GUTTA-PERCHA).

PERIODICAL PRINTING

Most book-collectors, being *book*-collectors, ignore magazines and newspapers which contain the first printing or a serialisation of something they want in first edition form. Thorough author-collectors take a sterner view of their responsibilities: some collect runs of periodicals for the sake of the serial, some extract the serial and have it bound. Even those who in general limit themselves to books allow a certain number of anomalous exceptions, mostly from among the border-line cases. For instance, Conan Doyle's *A Study in Scarlet* was first printed, in its entirety but amongst other contributions, in *Beeton's Christmas Annual* for 1887; and collectors have decided (quite illogically, but exercising their unquestioned right) to consider this the *desideratum*, rather than the first edition in book form (i.e. its first appearance between its own covers), which was published in the following year—and is, incidentally, about five times rarer today. More rational exceptions are such works as Rider Haggard's *Mr. Meeson's Will*, which occupied an entire issue of *The Illustrated London News* in 1888, or Evelyn Waugh's *The Loved One* (in *Horizon*, February 1948).

The Carl H. Pforzheimer Library: English Literature 1475–1700. New York, Privately Printed, 1940.

This bibliographically exhaustive 1300-quarto-page catalogue, which owes its quite special authority to its editor, William A. Jackson, is frequently cited simply by number. (cf. HAYWARD, ROTHSCHILD, SADLEIR)

PICTORIAL
(OF BOARDS, CLOTH OR WRAPPERS)

Until the 1850's, pictorial, as distinct from formal, decoration of boarded and wrappered books was executed in one colour, usually black on a coloured ground. (Gilt pictorial decoration on the spines of PUBLISHER'S CLOTH bindings was common enough in the late 1830's and the 1840's.) In 1853 an experiment in multi-coloured pictorial boards was made (*Letters left at the Pastry-Cook's*, by J. S. Mayhew), and this shortly ushered in the great spate of gaily boarded cheap books commonly known as YELLOW-BACKS.

A similar technique was soon applied to cloth, and though glazed pictorial cloth bindings were never as common as boarded or wrappered ones, they were in occasional use till the end of the century.

PIGSKIN

When tanned in the ordinary way, pigskin, as a leather for binding, is intractable and, though very tough, liable to get brittle for lack of grease. When tawed with alum, it is much more tractable and very durable. It does not lend itself to decoration, except in BLIND, and most pigskin bindings are rugged rather than elegant.

PIRATED EDITION, PIRACY

A term commonly applied (sometimes with, sometimes without, legal accuracy) to an edition produced and marketed without the authority of, or payment to, the author. Piracy has decreased with the development of international protection of author's copyright; but it is not unknown even today.

Aldus's texts (and IMPRINT) were freely copied in Lyons and elsewhere in the early 16th century. In the 17th and 18th, piracy was particularly brisk in books which for doctrinal or political reasons could not be licensed or otherwise protected or even avowed: Rochester, Swift and Defoe, Pascal, Rousseau and Voltaire provide well-known examples. In England in the 17th and 18th centuries the custom of circulating an author's work in manuscript offered plenty of opportunities to over-zealous friends or unscrupulous publishers, and in the 18th the booksellers of Edinburgh and Dublin waged open war on their tightly organised rivals in London. The 19th century was the heyday of transatlantic 'piracy'—a misnomer in this instance, for neither side could claim any legal protection from the other—and if the publishers of New York and Philadelphia made freer with English authors than London publishers did with American, it was only because Scott, Dickens or Hardy was more saleable there than Longfellow or Emerson here.

For an estimate of the current attitudes of collectors towards these various types of piracy, see AUTHORISED EDITION and 'FOLLOW THE FLAG'.

PLATE-MARK
The impression made in the leaf of paper by the edge of the metal plate used for printing engravings, etc. (see ILLUSTRATION PROCESSES).

PLATE-NUMBERS
The numbers (with or without initials) at the foot of the pages of engraved music, which indicate the numerical position of the score in its publisher's output and provide one of the few reliable clues to its original publication date.

PLATES
(1) Properly, plates are whole-sheet illustrations, printed separately from the text; e.g. 'plates spotted', 'with the rare extra plate of *Leda and the Swan*', 'lacks two of the twenty-four plates'. Illustrations printed on the text pages are

PLATES (continued)

called *cuts* (or, by printers, *figures*) unless they are described in greater detail (e.g. as engravings or woodcuts). But the distinction is not always observed.

See also ILLUSTRATION PROCESSES.

(2) STEREOTYPE or other such plates, used instead of type for text printing.

POINT SYSTEM
(OF TYPE)

A numerical system for the measurement and description of type sizes. The first version of this system was introduced by Fournier of Paris in 1737, and another by Didot at the end of the 18th century. A formula different from either of these was eventually adopted in England and America. A point is approximately one seventy-second of an inch. *This book is set in 11-point type.*

These antiseptic terms, ranging for book-work from 6-point to 30 or 36, have almost entirely superseded such traditional, romantically mysterious names as minion, ruby, nonpareil (pronounced nomprell), brevier (breveer), bourgeois (berjoice), long primer (rhymes with trimmer), pica (rhymes with Leica), canon and english.

POINTILLÉ

Gold-tooled decoration on leather bindings producing a dotted effect, whether by the repetition of single dots or by the use of TOOLS with dotted instead of solid outlines. (H. M. Nixon)

POINTS

A *point* is any peculiarity in a book whose presence in or absence from a particular copy calls for note. It is most often used of bibliographical peculiarities: the evidence (or alleged evidence) for priority of ISSUE, BINDING VARIANTS, MISPRINTS, variant ADVERTISEMENTS, CANCELS, textual changes, etc.

Some collectors hate, and a few despise, points. Others love them, as do most booksellers' cataloguers. For, as Richard Curle once said, 'Books without points are like women without beauty—they pass unnoticed in a crowd. But books with points excite immediate interest ... therefore there is an instinctive tendency to dwell on points, to exaggerate their significance [see POINT-MANIACS], and even to discover points that are not really points at all [see ISSUE-MONGERS]'.

This propensity takes three main forms in catalogue notes: (*a*) The *scholarly exposition* of the full details, with references to any relevant bibliographical authorities, perhaps some argument, and a conclusion or at least an inference. (*b*) The *dust-in-your-eye* technique: a lot of details impressively, or a few brusquely, set down, without explanation or references (or if with references, without indication whose side the quoted authority is on), FIRST ISSUE in large type—and the hope that readers will be too dazed to ask questions. (*c*) The *surely-I-don't-have-to-tell-you* line: this, which ingenuously (or disingenuously) assumes that collectors are familiar with all the reference books, consists of such airy notes as 'with the point on page 16', 'with all but one of the points called for by Heidsieck', or simply 'with all the points'.

The term is also sometimes used in contexts not strictly bibliographical; particularly of some factor in the condition of a book which experience has shown to be common to most copies. For instance, the *point* in Kepler *Astronomia Nova* 1609 is that the paper is almost always badly browned; in Sheridan *The Critic* 1781 that the half-title is almost always missing; in *The Old Wives' Tale* 1908 that the white lettering on the backstrip has almost always flaked off.

POINT-MANIACS

These are the collectors who do not merely love POINTS but love them to excess. A relish for bibliographical complexities and the agreeable consciousness of expertness induced by the successful unravelling of a technical problem are among the proper pleasures of connoisseurship. Their results will often contribute to the common stock of bibliographical knowledge; nor is it anything but estimable in a collector to like a tricky book (other things being equal) better than a straightforward one. But just as extreme degrees of rarity or doctrinaire attitudes towards condition have sometimes played havoc with the collector's sense of proportion, so has the passion for points.

For every experienced collector who can tell a legitimate point when he sees one, and can enjoy it for what it is worth and no more, there are ten young aspirants or humble late-comers to the pursuit who are all too ready to believe the numerous bibliographical fairy-tales which, in course of time, have become so familiar as to be repeated almost without thought. These innocents, rightly determined to master the technicalities of book-collecting, are the natural prey of ISSUE-MONGERS. Mesmerised by the magic words *First Edition* and thrilled by the realisation that there are also such things as first issues, first states, primary bindings and so forth, they fall easy victims to the CHRONOLOGICAL OBSESSION.

POST-INCUNABULA

Books of INCUNABULAR character printed after 1500—how long after, the experts have not yet agreed. This useful term was apparently coined by Wouter Nijhoff *c.* 1900, and in Holland (as perhaps elsewhere on the Continent) it means books printed 1501–1540. It was adopted twenty years later by Stephen Gaselee and is generally used in England for books printed 1501–1520.

PRE-FIRST

This self-contradictory term, having no proper meaning of its own, is put to various uses, many of them dubious, but all symptomatic of the CHRONOLOGICAL OBSESSION. It alleges that the edition, issue or copy referred to precedes the commonly accepted first edition; and *pre-first* may be found applied to TRIAL ISSUES, ADVANCE COPIES, COPYRIGHT editions, PRIVATELY PRINTED editions, PIRATED or unauthorised editions, EXTRACTS, OFFPRINTS, and even magazine appearances.

PRELIMINARY LEAVES, or PRELIMS

The leaves which precede the actual text, i.e. half-title, title, list of contents, dedication, preface, etc. They are usually the last to be printed, and are from their variable composition liable to irregularities of make-up, of pagination (if any) and of SIGNATURE (again, if any). Blank leaves which are integral to the first GATHERING count for bibliographical purposes as part of the prelims; but they are not always reckoned in the pagination, which is customarily (*though not in this book*) in roman numerals and is thus distinct from that of the main body of the text.

PRESENTATION BINDING

Used variously for GIFT BINDING or AUTHOR'S BINDING.

PRESENTATION COPY

When used without qualification, this may always be taken to mean that the book was the gift of the author. But only a book spontaneously presented properly qualifies for the description; one merely signed in response to an owner's request is called an INSCRIBED COPY.

It is useful to consider the various ways in which such gifts have been bestowed; for any one of them would be considered by a cataloguer to justify the description *presentation copy*, yet they arouse widely differing degrees of enthusiasm in the discriminating collector.

The pre-eminent quality in any presentation copy will always be that of its ASSOCIATION—the interest or importance of the recipient, his connexion with the author or other such special recommendation. This will override most of the niceties distinguishable in the method of presentation; but, assuming the interest of association to be constant, these may be roughly graded as follows:

(1) With a signed presentation inscription in the author's hand to a named recipient; dated before, on or near publication.

(2) Ditto; but undated or dated considerably later than publication.

(3) With the recipient's name, but having *from the author* or *with the author's compliments* instead of signature.

(4) Without autograph inscription, but showing evidence of having been sent by the author or on his instructions by the publisher. In 18th or early 19th century books the latter's clerk would write in some such phrase as those italicised in (3) above; in more modern books a printed or typed slip would be loosely inserted.

(5) With a note in the hand of the recipient stating that the book was the gift of the author.

(6) With a later note making a similar statement at second-hand, from family tradition or the like.

There are further subdivisions; and preference between (4) and (5) will be a matter of taste.

PRESS BOOKS

A jargon term, but a useful one, covering the products of (*a*) PRIVATE PRESSES proper, e.g. Strawberry Hill, Lee Priory, Eragny, Gregynog; (*b*) concerns which, though not printing houses, call themselves 'presses' because they specialise in fine book-production, e.g. Vale, Nonesuch; and sometimes (*c*) printers whose work is collected for its own sake, whether it was executed for a commercial publisher, e.g. Bulmer, Chiswick, Curwen, Bruce Rogers, or issued over their own imprint, e.g. Aldus, Estienne, Plantin, Baskerville. Class (*b*) does not include the publications of university presses, or of the fairly numerous publishing firms which choose to call themselves something which they are not.

PRESS FIGURES

Numerals, letters or symbols printed in the lower margins of many 18th century English books (and a few American), normally on the VERSO of the leaf and seldom therefore liable to be confused with SIGNATURES. (They are sometimes found in late 17th century and early 19th century English books—the Waverley novels are a well-known case.) Each press or pressman was assigned a mark, and these were used for computing piecework earnings. It seems likely that press figures may assist in the detection not only of otherwise undifferentiated re-impressions but also of HALF SHEET imposition and other problems of FORMAT, the size of editions, and the size and practice of particular printing shops. But until the analytical bibliographers deliver final judgment the collector will only need to bother his head with them in cases where they have been proved significant for a particular edition of some particular book.

PRESS-MARK

'In libraries, a mark or number [often both] written or stamped in or on each book, and also given in the library catalogue, specifying the room, book-press [hence the name], book-case, shelf, etc., where the book is kept' (SOED).

In private libraries these marks (often a combination of letters and numerals) are usually written inside the front cover, whether on a label or directly on the endpaper. They are sometimes called *shelf-marks*, *case-marks* or, if of the labelled variety, *case-labels*. In America they are usually known as *call-numbers*.

Seymour de Ricci, in his *English Collectors of Books and Manuscripts*, shows how much can be learned from the study of press-marks by anyone concerned with the PROVENANCE of books.

PRIMARY BINDING

A term used to distinguish the earliest of any different publisher's binding styles found on copies of the same edition from later ones (SECONDARY or REMAINDER). It is only applicable to EDITION-BOUND books, and in practice is seldom used of anything except PUBLISHER'S CLOTH; though it would be correctly applied to a boards-and-label copy of a book published between 1820 and 1830 if later-issued copies were known to have been put up in gilt-lettered cloth (i.e. after 1832).

PRINTER'S MARK
See DEVICE.

PRIVATE PRESS

A private press is one whose owner or operator prints what he likes, how he likes, not what a publisher pays him to print. He may, and usually does, sell his products to the public, whether directly to subscribers or through the booksellers, or, occasionally, through a publisher's organisation. But he is out to make a fine book rather than a profit. He may employ a printer, as Horace Walpole did at Strawberry Hill, or he may conduct the press himself, like Robert Gibbings at the Golden Cockerel. But he decides what to print and how it shall be printed.

As generally understood, the term *private press* would be applied only to a shop where the work was hand-set and hand-printed. Its editions are likely to be strictly limited in size.

PRIVATELY PRINTED

This term seldom means what it says, viz. that the *printing* was actually carried out in a privy manner. It can refer to the product of a PRIVATE PRESS; but it is generally used of something *not published*: that is, something produced not to the order, nor at the expense, of a publisher, but for the author, or one of his friends or patrons, or even a zealous stranger, and thereafter privately circulated, or distributed by other than the usual commercial methods. Alternatively, the description may be used by a publisher for some book which, if published in the ordinary way, might expose him the more readily to legal penalties on the ground of libel or obscenity.

This need not imply that the book was necessarily given away. Indeed, the announcement that something has been *privately printed* or is to be *printed for private circulation only* was found, at least as early as the 18th century, to attract collectors; and it still does.

Books or pamphlets produced for genuinely private distribution are apt to be genuinely scarce, even if they were not, as often, printed in a very small number. If they were printed for the author to give away, the proportion of PRESENTATION COPIES is likely to be much higher than with a regularly published book.

PRIVILEGE, PRIVILEGE LEAF

In the days before the Copyright Act of 1709 a printer or publisher would sometimes secure from the competent authority a *privilege* (often, but not necessarily, a monopoly) for the printing of a particular book or class of books within the area of the authority's jurisdiction; usually for a limited period, but sometimes for the duration of his office as printer by appointment to the said authority or another, or even for life. This would be signalised either by some such phrase as *Cum Privilegio*, printed on the title-page or above the COLOPHON, or by a more extended pronouncement, often printed on a separate leaf, usually at the beginning of the book. There are occasional post-1700 examples.

Cf. IMPRIMATUR.

PROCTOR

Index to the Early Printed Books in the British Museum: with Notes of those in the Bodleian Library, by Robert Proctor, 1898, etc. Supplements, index by Konrad Burger, continuation by F. S. Isaac, 1938. Reprint, 1960.

The principles of comparative anatomy and the analogies of natural history were first adapted to the historical classification of books by Henry Bradshaw (1831–86) of Cambridge. But they were applied on a large scale to early printed books by a younger bibliographer, Robert Proctor (1868–1903). The result was *Proctor's order*: the classification of early printed books on scientific typographical principles by country, town and printer. And although Proctor's own work will be less often referred to as BMC nears completion, it is fitting that both the writer and the readers of the present handbook should pay tribute to the memory of one of the greatest of INCUNABULISTS.

PROOFS BEFORE LETTERS

A term used to describe proofs of engravings, etc., taken (sometimes on special paper) before the addition of caption, imprint, date or other matter.

Of the more ambitious illustrated books of the late 18th and early 19th centuries there was sometimes a special issue, at a considerably advanced price, with the text on

large or fine paper and 'proof impressions of the plates'.
These would often be *proofs before letters*.

PROOFS, PROOF COPIES

First proofs of a book (see also GALLEYS) are provided by
the printer for the author's correction and the publisher's
scrutiny. Revised proofs are the intermediate stage either
to final proofs or, if these are dispensed with, to the finished
book. The author's set (or sets) of proofs are apt to carry
marginal corrections, additions, etc., in his own hand,
varying from a few words to rewritten paragraphs. Of
the revised or the final proofs (usually stitched and
wrappered), the 20th century publisher will commonly
order a quite large number, for use in the office and in the
promotion of the book; and whereas the bibliographical
distinction between wrappered final proofs and ADVANCE
COPIES is significant, the physical differences are often
slight.

Except for specialist author-collectors, to whom every
embryonic stage of a book has some interest, and unless it
is known that substantial excisions were made at the proof
stage, collectors tend to distinguish sharply between proofs
annotated by the author himself—the half-way stage
between his manuscript or typescript and the first edition
—and those others, often numerous, which bear at most
the routine markings of the printer's or publisher's reader
and in many cases no markings at all.

PROVENANCE

The pedigree of a book's previous ownership. This may
be clearly marked by the owner's name, arms, bookplate,
or other evidence in the book itself; it may be less clearly
indicated by PRESS-MARKS; or it may have to be pieced
together from such outside sources as auction records or
booksellers' catalogues. Apart from such special features
in a book's provenance as might put it in the category of
an ASSOCIATION COPY, the evidences of its earlier history
are always of interest (documentary or sentimental) and
sometimes of importance. They should never be destroyed,

deleted or tampered with, but on the contrary cherished—and added to.

Nor should this respect for a book's history be denied to the notes (including code marks) of booksellers through whose hands it has passed. It is not nothing that a Renaissance text stood once on the shelves of Ludwig Rosenthal or E. Ph. Goldschmidt or Leo S. Olschki or Lathrop Harper. And the collector who has just finished COLLATING a newly acquired Elizabethan quarto knows that he is in honourable company when he adds his mark to the pencilled note on the back ENDPAPER: 'Collated and perfect. Bernard Quaritch Ltd' (especially if the note happens to be initialled F.S.F., which stands for a Past President and Gold Medallist of the Bibliographical Society).

Provenance is interesting in proportion to the interest of the previous owners, whether as contemporary with its publication, or as persons of importance in their own right, or because they were book-collectors of note. It may be important, in the appraisal of an outstanding or very rare book, either as identifying it with one of x copies known, or for the guarantee of quality bestowed on it by having belonged to a respected connoisseur.

In most cases the cataloguer's reference to a book's provenance will be in straightforward form: e.g. 'De Thou's copy, with his arms on the binding impaled with those of his second wife', 'From Richard Heber's library, with his stamp', 'The Wodhull copy, with notes in his hand on the fly-leaf', 'The Renouard-Corser-Ashburnham copy'. But a handful of famous libraries are commonly known by the name not of the owner but of his or his family's residence; thus Syston Park means the Thorold family, Britwell means Christie Miller, Hamilton Palace means almost certainly William Beckford, Rowfant means Frederick Locker, White Knights means the fifth Duke of Marlborough, better known to book-collectors as the Marquess of Blandford, Ashley means Thomas J. Wise.

The generally laudable attention paid to provenance (which Americans sometimes, and regrettably, over-anglicise into the bogus word *provenience*) is occasionally pushed to a length which, if not in itself slightly ridiculous, has of recent years begun to be indiscriminate. To salute 'The Coningsby-Locksley Hall–Hentzau–Casamassima–D'Urberville copy' is one thing: to dress up some mediocre volume with the note that it is 'The Black–White–Green–Brown–Gray copy' is another. A pedigree is not always distinguished just because it is long.

PUBLICATION

'The issuing or offering to the public, of a book, map, engraving, piece of music, etc.; also the work or business of producing and issuing copies of such works, 1576. (*b*) A work published; a book or the like printed or otherwise produced and issued for public sale, 1656'. Thus SOED. And notwithstanding that COPYRIGHT EDITIONS, books PRIVATELY PRINTED or books issued only to SUBSCRIBERS are reckoned by collectors as the first editions of the works concerned, the crucial factor in publication remains the offering of the book, for sale, to the public.

In the eyes of the English law the fact of publication is established not by REGISTRATION at Stationers' Hall, nor by the deposit of a copy of the book at the British Museum (the principal COPYRIGHT LIBRARY), but by the evidence of copies being sold, or openly offered for sale, to the public. And publication day, the day on which that offering for sale is first generally made, is the decisive moment for subsequent collectors of first editions. For the copies of a book made available on that day represent the finished product (as distinct from such pre-publication, or chrysalis, stages as PROOFS, ADVANCE COPIES, TRIAL ISSUES, etc.), but the product in its first, pristine form before the possible incidence of such things as second ISSUES, SECONDARY BINDINGS or other afterthoughts. Publication day is, bibliographically, the book's D-day.

PUBLISHER'S CLOTH

The use of cloth for EDITION-BINDING by the publisher dates from about 1823. It had become general in English and American publishing by 1835, except for poetry and other slender volumes, and (for special reasons) fiction. It has been almost universal for new books of any bulk since about 1850. Originally introduced as a novelty alternative to the prevailing paper-covered BOARDS, and like them conceived of as a mere temporary covering until the book should be leather-bound, its possibilities as a permanent binding had become clear by the early 1830s; and although many purchasers of books issued in publisher's cloth continued to have them bound before putting them on their shelves, the number of these has grown steadily smaller.

Edition-binding in cloth, once it was established, meant that the publisher assumed a part of the final cost of a book which had in previous centuries been borne by the purchaser, whether on his own binder's bill or in the extra price charged for copies bound by the retail or wholesale bookseller. For the collector, it meant the establishment of a uniform original binding functionally inseparable from the book within it and readily identifiable, if not on sight, at least by comparison with other copies of the same edition.

For books of earlier date there is room for difference of opinion among collectors united in their insistence on ORIGINAL STATE, for the sound reason (discussed under that entry and under TRADE BINDING) that positive identification of an original binding is seldom possible. But once the hunter's quarry are dressed in uniforms, there is no mistaking them, even though there may be significant changes in their insignia or other details (see SECONDARY BINDINGS). And it has become an established convention that no book issued in publisher's cloth should be admitted to the fastidious collector's library in any other dress. Exception would be made for PRESENTATION or ASSOCIATION copies, and (by any except fanatics) for books so rare that even a re-bound copy may present the only chance of a lifetime. But the exceptions are few.

QUARTER BOUND

A book with leather back (spine), sides covered with cloth

QUARTER BOUND (continued)

or paper, and no leather corners, is said to be *quarter bound*.

See also HALF BOUND, HALF CLOTH, ROXBURGHE STYLE.

QUARTO

A book essentially squarish in shape and normally lying between folio and octavo in size, though varying considerably in this respect. The telephone directory is a typical large quarto, yet it is twice the page-area of the average Jacobean quarto play.

For details see FORMAT.

QUIRE

When used as a bibliographical term, this is synonymous with a GATHERING or section. (Publishers nowadays use it also to mean the flat, unfolded sheets. To a paper-maker it means one-twentieth of a ream of paper.)

RAISED BANDS

In normal European and American practice, when a book is bound (as distinct from being CASED), the gathered sections are sewn on to horizontal cords or bands, usually four or five in number, the ends of which are then laced into the boards. When the boards are covered, these cords (unless sunk in grooves to make a smooth spine) will stand out in the form of ridges. These are known as *raised bands*. In most leather-bound books their presence is taken for granted; and they will only be mentioned in a catalogue description (*a*) if it is an unusually detailed and elaborate one, or (*b*) if, as in some leather-*cased* modern books, the 'raised bands' are bogus, non-functional excrescences added to suggest genuine binding.

RARITY

Rarity is the salt in book-collecting. But if you take too much salt, the flavour of the dish is spoiled; and if you take it neat it will make you sick. Similarly, those book-collectors who exalt rarity above any other criterion tend to develop third-degree bibliomania, which is a painful and slightly ridiculous ailment.

A. W. Pollard once defined book-collecting as 'the bringing together of books which in their contents, their form or the history of the individual copy possess some element of permanent interest, and either actually or prospectively are rare, in the sense of being difficult to procure. This qualification of rarity [he continued], which figures much too largely in the popular view of book-collecting, is entirely subordinate to that of interest, for the rarity of a book devoid of interest is a matter of no concern. On the other hand, so long as a book (or anything else) is and appears likely to continue to be easily procurable at any moment, no one has any reason for collecting it. The anticipation that it will always be easily procurable is often unfounded; but so long as the anticipation exists it restrains collecting.' *(Encyclopædia Britannica.)*

The definition of 'a rare book' is a favourite parlour game among bibliophiles. Paul Angle's 'important, desirable and hard to get' has been often and deservedly quoted: Robert H. Taylor's impromptu, 'a book I want badly and can't find', is here quoted for the first time.

As rarity is an important factor in book-collecting, it is useful to distinguish between its various kinds and to attempt an appraisal of its different degrees. Among the former are:

(1) *Absolute Rarity.* A property possessed by any book printed in a very small edition; of which therefore the total number of copies which could possibly survive is definitely known to be very small. For instance, of Horace Walpole *Hieroglyphic Tales* 1785 seven copies were printed, six of Tennyson *The Lover's Tale* 1833, and of Robert Frost *Twilight* [1894] only two.

(2) *Relative Rarity.* A property only indirectly connected with the number of copies printed. It is based on the number which survive, its practical index is the frequency of occurrence in the market, and its interest is the relation of this frequency to public demand.

(3) *Temporary Rarity.* This is due either to an inadequate supply of copies in the market of a book only recently begun to be collected, or to a temporary shortage of copies of an established favourite.

(4) *Localised Rarity*. This applies to books sought for outside the area of their original circulation or later popularity with collectors.

The First Folio Shakespeare and the Gutenberg Bible are certainly 'rare books' as the term is generally understood; yet scores of books which have also been actively collected for a century or so, and whose degree of rarity is therefore a matter of record, are much rarer than either. The original editions of *Tottel's Miscellany* 1557 and Shakespeare *Venus and Adonis* 1593, for instance, survive in only one copy apiece; and of the first book printed in Italy, the Subiaco *Donatus* of 1464, no copy has yet been recovered. But a book which no one has ever thought of looking for—and therefore no one else has troubled to preserve or remember—is often as difficult to find, and thus as rare in practical terms, as many expensive and notorious rarities. 'Tenth editions', said Charles Lamb, 'are scarcer than first editions'.

The study of comparative scarcities, pioneered by Michael Sadleir, is still in its infancy; and it cannot be pursued in an ABC.[1] The reliability of estimates of rarity attached to a particular book can be checked, at least partially, against its auction record and a comprehensive file of appropriate booksellers' catalogues. But the collector unfortified by experience of his own in searching for the book over any considerable period will often have to depend on the experience of others—sometimes represented by the bookseller who offers him a copy. And he will, in this as in so many other matters, trust those whom he has found sober as well as expert, while keeping a pinch of salt handy for the enthusiastic or the flighty.

The degrees of rarity attributed to books are expressed in a wide range of terms, mostly self-explanatory. These may have an appearance of precision; e.g. 'no copy sold at auction since 1902' or 'GKW records only seven copies', or 'only one copy in U.S.A., according to GOFF or STC', or

---

[1]The present writer pursued it through an entire chapter of *Taste and Technique in Book-Collecting* without grasping more than a few tail-feathers.

'unknown to Bollinger' (the bibliographer of the author). They may be related to the book's condition; e.g. 'very rare in boards', or 'uncommonly found in fine state', or 'almost all known copies are badly browned'. They may run simply from *scarce* to *very scarce* to *rare* to *very rare* to *exceedingly* or *notoriously rare* to *unrecorded and apparently unique*. But it must always be remembered that neither records nor bibliographers are infallible; that estimates based on experience depend on the width, length and acuteness of the experience; and finally that the delicate nuances between the terms used for expressing degrees of rarity vary between one user and another.

READING COPY
A usually apologetic but occasionally slightly defiant term meaning that the book is not in collector's condition. A reading copy will probably look worse than a SECOND-HAND COPY but better than a WORKING COPY.

RE-BACKED
This means that the binding of the book has been given a new backstrip or spine. It is mostly used of leather-bound or boarded or wrappered books, for this often necessary but usually unsightly form of repair is seldom resorted to for publisher's cloth. Unless otherwise stated (e.g. 'original boards re-backed with cloth', 'contemporary calf re-backed with morocco'), it may be assumed that the new back is of similar material to the old.

Re-backed is usually distinct from RE-JOINTED. But when some part of the old backstrip has been salvaged and mounted on the new, a sort of hybrid between the two is created. The catalogue description will normally give particulars of this: e.g. 'old calf, re-backed, portions of the original backstrip preserved', or 'boards, re-backed, original label (defective) laid down'. Apart from labels (whether leather or paper), it is seldom thought worth preserving less than a substantial portion of the old back in this way, with the result that these hybrids are apt to resemble re-jointed books, which they are not, rather than re-backed ones, which (underneath it all) they are.

A book which, being shaken or loose, has been taken out of its covers and re-settled in them more firmly is said to be re-cased. Glue, probably some re-sewing and often new ENDPAPERS, will be involved in this operation, which is performed on twenty cloth books for every one in leather. For a leather-bound book in a similar state of disrepair is more apt for RE-JOINTING or RE-BACKING, though if the covers are intact it may be RE-SET.

Most re-casing is not hard to detect: the spine often looks too tight, the book opens stiffly, the covers have either a slightly scrubbed or a slightly glazed look, the endpapers (even if they are the original ones) do not lie quite flat, the top edges have sometimes been scraped, a fresh strip of paper glued down the back of the sewn gatherings may be visible if the book is opened wide. But an expert job may be very difficult to detect, even if one is suspicious, which one sometimes forgets to be.

Suspicion on this point should in fact be unceasing. For there are a much larger number of re-cased books about than most collectors (or even all booksellers) realise; and whereas it is a matter of judgment whether to prefer an entirely untouched copy in slightly shaken condition to another which is sound because it has been re-cased, it has always to be remembered that once a book and its case have been divorced, only the owner and the binder concerned know whether they were remarried to the same partners.

Since the second edition of, for example, *The Woman in White*, or *Great Expectations*, or *Trilby*, was published in a binding indistinguishable from the first, a copy of the first edition which is clean inside but damaged as to its binding can be placed in the covers of a brilliant copy of the second just as easily as it can be replaced in its own. And since the difference in market value between a fine copy of the first edition and a fine copy of the second is in a proportion (for such are first edition collectors) of perhaps twenty to one, it will be seen that the temptation to perform such switching operations may be powerful.

That is an extreme case. But it is the knowledge of his own uncertainty as to what may have been done to a re-cased copy that makes the wary and the fastidious collector prefer almost any other.

RECTO

The front, or obverse, side of the leaf; i.e. the right-hand page of an open book or manuscript. Its complement is the *verso*.

REGISTER

(1) In the early days of printing the printer would sometimes provide, usually on the last page just above the COLOPHON but occasionally on a separate leaf, a list of the SIGNATURE-letters and a note of the composition of the GATHERINGS in the book, for the guidance of the binder. This list is known as the *register*.

(2) 'Registered on 16 May 1605', or the like, refers to the entering of a copyright in the Register of the Stationers' Company. This practice, never regular (or legally necessary, except under the Licensing Act of 1662), decreased steadily during the 18th and 19th centuries and has become obsolete since the Copyright Act of 1911.

(3) Printers use the term to mean the exact fit of matter printed on the same page in more than one operation of the press (e.g. if illustrations or coloured initials are printed separately from the text). Thus an initial or a vignette may be described as 'out of register'. It is also used of the correspondence of type-area on the two sides of the sheet.

RE-HINGED

See RE-JOINTED.

RE-ISSUE

A term even more indefinite than REPRINT. It may imply a later ISSUE of the original book, substantially unchanged, but with a new title-page or a different binding. It may imply a new IMPRESSION, with or without similar changes. Or it may imply an entirely new EDITION: e.g. 'the book was later re-issued in pocket size'.

RE-JOINTED

When the JOINTS of a book have deteriorated through the stages of *rubbed*, *tender* and *weak*, to being more than merely 'slightly' defective, its owner may decide to have it re-jointed. If the damage has not gone too far and if the binder is skilful, this can be done so neatly as to be hardly perceptible on the shelf—and occasionally even in the hand. Cataloguers are, on the whole, fairly conscientious in recording any except the most invisible re-jointing; but none worth his salt would omit a reassuring adjective of some kind. Thus, a workmanlike job will usually be described as *skilful* or *almost imperceptible*, while even cobbler's work is likely to be promoted to *neat*.

Re-jointing, however well executed, is of some import to collectors who set a high value on ORIGINAL STATE (if the copy was in such state) and of much more import, for visual reasons, to sticklers for fine condition. Unless the book is very rare or the copy very badly battered, the former will think twice before sacrificing their cherished quality to mere soundness. The latter will probably not think once.

REMAINDER BINDING

When a book has virtually ceased to sell, its publisher may dispose of his moribund stock to a wholesaler or bookseller for whatever it will fetch. This is called *remaindering*. The buyer then markets it at a reduced price. If, as normally in the 19th century (and sometimes even today), the remainder consists not of bound copies but of unbound QUIRES or even unfolded SHEETS, he will have to bind them; and it stands to reason that he will do so as economically as he can. This results in a *remainder binding*, which may differ considerably from the publisher's. Two- and three-volume works, for instance, were sometimes remainder-bound in one volume.

For 19th and 20th century books, the term *remainder binding* is properly applicable only to EDITION-BINDING demonstrably executed to the order of, or for wholesale marketing by, someone other than the book's original publisher. Later (and sometimes cheaper) bindings of his own are called SECONDARY BINDINGS.

RE-MARGINED

When one or more of the three outer margins of a leaf has been restored, it is said to be re-margined. If it is the inner margin only, the proper term is EXTENDED. If all four margins have had to be renewed, the leaf is described as INLAID.

REMBOÎTAGE

There ought to be, but is not, an English word for this. The practice may be commoner in France than in England, but not all that commoner. RE-CASING is the nearest term, but that does not of itself suggest that the book has been put back in any covers but its own.

Remboîtage means the transferring of a book from its own binding to another more elegant, more nearly contemporary, more appropriate—anyway, more desirable; or, alternatively, the transferring into a superior binding of a text more interesting or valuable than the one for which it was made. This often involves a new LETTERING-PIECE (the leather label); but even so, if it has been skilfully executed, it is sometimes difficult to detect.

REPAIRING AND RESTORATION

Some of the more drastic measures of repair and restoration are touched upon under such entries as RE-BACKED, RE-JOINTED, RE-CASED, MADE-UP, RE-MARGINED, EXTENDED, INLAID, MOUNTED, WASHED. But whether the collector has to decide on accepting or rejecting a copy already restored, or is considering having one of his own books repaired, there are a great many minor operations to be taken into account as well as these. The patching of torn or defective margins, the supplying of a missing endpaper or lettering-piece, the re-covering of sides whose marbled or plain paper is badly worn or torn, the filling of wormholes, the ironing out of dog-eared or creased leaves—all these and many similar measures may either have already been taken or may seem to be called for.

REPAIRING AND RESTORATION (continued)

The greatly increased respect for ORIGINAL STATE among collectors of the present century has tended to reduce to the minimum the amount of tampering with even battered copies that most of them will tolerate, let alone procure, in England or America today. (The French take a very different line.) And current convention excuses defects in a copy which can truthfully be described as *entirely untouched* much more readily than it finds merits in one which has been furbished into brightness.

Possibly, indeed, this healthy reaction from the indiscriminate repairing and rebinding practised by our forefathers has gone a little too far. A repaired book is not necessarily a doctored, sophisticated or faked-up book, even though examples of the latter are still quite plentiful enough to make us wary. And the collector who keeps his eyes open when buying one, or gives his own job to a reliable binder (*and* makes a note in it afterwards of what has been done), has no need to apologise to anyone.

REPRINT

A term used loosely for either a new edition or a new impression from the same setting-up of type (see EDITION AND IMPRESSION).

RE-SET

(1) When a leaf or leaves, or a whole section, has come loose from the binding and has been stuck back again, usually with paste or glue, it is said to be re-set.

(2) If the whole book is so shaken and loose as to be unserviceable, it may be re-set in its binding. (See also RE-CASED.)

(3) A printer re-sets *type* for a new edition, or for a new leaf for insertion in an existing one—e.g. 'first edition, but the ISSUE with the title-page re-set'.

REVERSE

(OF A LEAF)

The back side, often called the VERSO.

REVIEW COPIES, SLIPS, STAMPS

Review copies, sent out before publication, were in the 19th century sometimes marked by a written note on the endpaper or fly-leaf, sometimes by a printed slip loosely inserted and seldom surviving (the earliest example known to me dates from 1834). The latter method is almost universal today. But some early 20th century publishers marked copies sent for review with stamps, either inked, perforating or BLIND, usually placed on the title-page. Some collectors regard this as a defacement, like a library or ownership stamp. Others cheerfully accept the defacement, because it is evidence that the copy is of the earliest issue.

RINGS
(IN THE AUCTION ROOM)

A ring is any group of two or more persons (normally, but not necessarily, dealers) who agree together before a sale to refrain from bidding against each other, in order subsequently to share between themselves the saving, in cost price under the hammer, effected by this elimination of competition. The lots purchased by one or another of the ring's representatives are then re-auctioned in private, the difference between the two totals being divided among the members of the ring. This private auction is called the *settlement* or *knock-out*, and each man's share of the total price difference is called the *dividend*.

The anticipation of this communal credit-balance, which may often be substantial, also strengthens the hand of the ring's representatives in discouraging outside competitors in the early stages of a sale. For whereas a single bookseller would find it expensive to bid a succession of lots up to the ceiling—thus suggesting that the outsider had better stick to bookshops or retire to stamp-collecting—the cost of such action is shared by all members of the ring, who will jointly benefit from the resulting peace and quiet.

It will be seen that rings work very much like any other cartel. They are routine practice in many Continental countries (the French word is *la révision*). They have never flourished in the United States. Common if not general in

England during the 19th and early 20th centuries, they were made illegal by Act of Parliament in 1927, and thereafter dwindled to minimal proportions in the London sale-rooms. In 1956 they were formally denounced by the Antiquarian Booksellers' Association and participation in a ring is now forbidden to its members. Opinions vary as to their prevalence at country sales in Great Britain today.

ROAN
A thin, soft kind of sheepskin used by binders as a cheap substitute for MOROCCO from about 1790 onwards. Not at all durable, and seldom elegant even when well preserved.

ROLL
A binder's term, meaning originally a tool having a continuous or repeated design engraved round the edge of a wheel; and by extension the impression made by this on the leather. E.g. 'roll-tooled PANEL in gold' or 'decorated with BLIND rolls'.

ROMANESQUE
(OF BINDING)
Weale first described, and G. D. Hobson subsequently christened (*English Bindings before 1500*, 1929), this 'family' of 12th and early 13th century bindings, of which over a hundred examples have by now been recorded. Always of leather, usually dark brown, they were decorated with repeated impressions of figured metal TOOLS. The finest examples are French or English; but the style, distinct from the earlier Ottonian and the later Gothic, was also prevalent in Germany (though not in Spain or Italy).

ROMANTIQUE STYLE
(OF BINDING)
A loose expression embracing the more elaborate BLOCK-produced bindings, especially those with polychrome decoration, executed in France between *c.* 1815 and *c.* 1840, including bindings in the CATHEDRAL style.

A Catalogue of the Collection of Eighteenth-Century Printed Books and Manuscripts formed by Lord Rothschild. Privately printed, 1954.

The Rothschild catalogue, prepared by Miss N. M. Shawyer under the general supervision of John Hayward ('my faithful and patient mentor', as Lord Rothschild describes him in the foreword), is nowadays frequently cited simply by number (cf. HAYWARD, SADLEIR) whether for a book whose author has no bibliography of his own or for more up-to-date particulars provided for one who has.

ROUGH or REVERSED CALF

Rough, or reversed, calf, used for reference books, music scores, working manuals and the like since the 18th century, wears the inside of the skin outside, unpolished.

ROXBURGHE STYLE

Originally designed for the publications of the Roxburghe Club, founded by a group of patrician bibliophiles after the Duke of Roxburghe's sale in 1812, this special style of binding has a gilt-lettered smooth leather spine, usually brown or green, and dark-red paper-board sides, with no leather corners. It is, in fact, a QUARTER BINDING with a distinctive colour-scheme.

ROYAL BINDINGS

A book described as being in a 'royal binding' may be expected to have a sovereign's arms on one or both covers; but it must not necessarily be supposed that it therefore has a royal PROVENANCE. Such bindings are not uncommon, especially on books of the 16th and 17th centuries; for since very early days and until nearly a century ago, English binders used the royal arms quite indiscriminately as decoration. The BLIND-stamped bindings of King Henry VIII's reign, for instance, which are embellished with panels of the royal arms, are all TRADE BINDINGS. So are almost all the plain calf bindings bearing the arms of

Queen Elizabeth or her crowned falcon badge. Large prayer-books or Bibles with the royal arms may have come from one of the Royal Chapels—but they may equally well have come from any loyal parish church.

Except, therefore, for an occasional refugee from the British Museum, to which George II presented the Old Royal Library and George III most of his own collection, the odds are against any book with the royal arms which is today in the market ever having actually belonged to a King or a Queen of England. The onus of proof is on the cataloguer.

ROYAL PAPER COPY

Cf. IMPERIAL PAPER COPY. An 18th and early 19th century term for LARGE or FINE paper, used for special copies.

RUBBED

Rubbed and its polite synonym *chafed* are the equivalent of what the French call *fatigué*. If the BACKSTRIP or the JOINTS of a copy are described in a catalogue as *rubbed*, they will not necessarily be weak, but they are probably well on the way to it; and if the binding is of leather, they will be in need of resuscitation.

RUBRIC, RUBRICATED, RUBRISHER

A *rubric* is a heading to a chapter or section written or printed in red (with a specialised meaning in liturgical books). *Rubricated*, as used in descriptions of MSS. or early printed books, generally means that initial capitals and/or paragraph marks have been painted in red. The *rubricator* or *rubrisher* (a noun undeservedly obsolete) was the man who did the painting. Cf. ILLUMINATED, MINIATURE.

Rubricated is also sometimes, but wrongly, used of books correctly described as *ruled in red* (borders, underlining of words on the title-page, etc.), a common practice in the 16th and 17th centuries.

RUNNING TITLE
See HEADLINE

RUSSIA LEATHER

Cowhide tanned by a special process, giving it a rich, smooth effect; and impregnated with birch-bark oil, whence its characteristic scent. Russia leather was introduced from Muscovy before 1700 and applied to bookbinding soon after. Normally DICED, it was particularly popular with English binders between 1780 and 1830. But it is apt to fail at the joints, and it is not much used today.

SABIN

Bibliotheca Americana, a Dictionary of Books relating to America from its Discovery to the Present Time. Begun by Joseph Sabin, continued by Wilberforce Eames, and completed by R. W. G. Vail, New York, 1868–1936, 29 vols. Also a recent reprint. This is the most comprehensive reference book for AMERICANA.

SADLEIR

Michael Sadleir, XIX Century Fiction, A Bibliographical Record based on his own collection, 1952.

This catalogue of Sadleir's famous and comprehensive collection (now in the library of the University of California at Los Angeles) is nowadays commonly cited simply by number, whether (for prestige purposes) in addition to that of the author-bibliography, if any, or (often) because there is no individual bibliography of the author concerned.

SCORED CALF

CALF treated by a squeezing process which produces a crinkled effect, resembling a coarse STRAIGHT-GRAIN MOROCCO. Popular with English binders during the first thirty years of the 19th century, less popular since.

SCRIPTS

In descriptions of old manuscripts, the text hand will be identified in more or less detail according to the importance of the MS. and the scholarship of the cataloguer. Among the main classes of script are uncial, semi-uncial, insular, cursive, humanistic, round, Gothic, secretary; among the more specialised, Carolingian, Beneventan, *textus prescissus, cancellaresca* (chancery), etc.

Any reader who expects to find analyses of these and the many other hands in an unillustrated ABC is asking too much. He is referred, in the first instance, to the articles in the *Encyclopædia Britannica* on Palæography (the study of ancient hand-writing) by A. de Brouard, and on Calligraphy (the art of fine writing) by Stanley Morison, both of which are furnished with full bibliographies.

SECONDARY BINDING

Publishers are seldom so confident of a book's success that they bind up at once the whole number of copies printed. They order further bindings-up in accordance with sales and estimated needs; and a slow-selling book may be bound in batches over a period of years. This practice was more widespread, and the periods involved were much longer, in the 19th century than today: and EDITION-BINDING has become increasingly mechanised and standardised. Consequently, BINDING VARIANTS—slight (or substantial) differences between one batch and the next—are commoner in 19th century books than in 20th.

Often there will be no visible difference between the 500 copies bound in, say, 1871 and the 250 bound in 1872; so that though the latter form strictly a later ISSUE, the collector will be spared any knowledge of it. If the copy, though identical in binding, is betrayed by late ADVERTISEMENTS—whether printed on the endpapers or an inserted catalogue—as being one of a binding-up which cannot have been the first, this is still a subdivision of the PRIMARY binding, though a less desirable one. For there is no physical difference in the binding itself.

When there is such a difference, the result is a secondary binding; a category which, in current usage, includes any further binding variants recorded on copies of the same edition, unless there is evidence that one of them is a REMAINDER binding. Even if the publisher makes no intentional change—of colour, of decoration, of fabric, for economy, or (very occasionally) for additional attraction—the binder may employ a different IMPRINT die (of several in use for this particular publisher's work), the cloth used before may be out of stock, or some other minor difference may be introduced.

When such variants have been identified, those interested in the book who are concerned to be sure that they have it in its earliest form, must decide (if they can) which represents the first, or primary, and which the later binding or bindings (secondaries). And if anyone suspects that this whole business is less simple than it has been made to sound here, he may confirm it by reference to the present writer's *Binding Variants in English Publishing, 1820–1900* (1932) and *More Binding Variants* (1938), where a number of particularly poisonous examples are examined in detail.

SECOND-HAND COPY

Far from fine, often neither very sound nor very clean, probably better than poor or DEFECTIVE, and certainly better than a READING, let alone a WORKING, copy. *A good second-hand copy*, in short, means that the condition is respectable but not much more.

SECTION

A synonym for a GATHERING: used mostly in such phrases as 'a clean copy, but two sections loose', or 'one section badly opened'.

SEMIS, SEMÉ

A binding term, from heraldry, meaning sprinkled or dotted (literally, sown) with small ornaments.

SERIALS, SERIALISATION

The practice of *re*printing fiction in serial form in periodicals dates from the beginning of the 18th century, *Robinson Crusoe* in *The London Post*, 1719–20, being an early example. The earliest novel *first* published in instalments seems to have been *The Adventures of Sir Launcelot Greaves*, by Tobias Smollett, which appeared during 1760 and 1761 in *The British Magazine*. It was only in the second quarter of the 19th century that the latter, and to collectors far more significant, practice became widespread; but of the output of popular novelists writing since that date it is probable that something between one third and one half was first published in serial form. (In the 19th century what we call PART-ISSUES were sometimes called serials.)

Mr. Graham Pollard, who has given us the best short account of serial fiction publishing,[1] made a telling case against its general neglect by collectors who profess to be seeking the earliest printed form of the books of their choice. Yet except among the more devoted author-collectors, it continues to be neglected; and the first appearance in book form, i.e. the 'first edition' as commonly understood, remains the general collector's *desideratum*. It is likely that more attention will be paid to magazine texts as it is more widely realised how often and how considerably they differ from the subsequent book-text. Yet runs of magazines (containing much alien matter) are troublesome to shelve even when assembled; and bound-up extracts from the run (the alien matter discarded) still lack the continuity of a book.

SEWN, SEWED, STITCHED

When followed by the confirmatory phrase 'as issued', these terms, used of pamphlets, offprints, slender volumes of verse and the like, mean that the GATHERING or gatherings of which they are composed have been sewn vertically in the regular way (as distinct from being STABBED or STAPLED), but no more; i.e. the item has not been bound, cased, boarded or even wrappered, but was issued naked.

Sewn, sewed used alone is more often synonymous with UNBOUND.

SHAKEN, SHAKY

Used mostly of books in PUBLISHER'S CLOTH, and meaning that the book itself is no longer firm in its covers. A copy described as *shaken* will almost always have given way at the inside hinges, but it need not be expected to be positively loose.

[1] In *New Paths in Book-Collecting*, 1934; later re-issued separately in Messrs. Constable's *Aspects of Book-Collecting* series. See also R. M. Wiles's *Serial Publication in England before 1750*, Cambridge, 1957.

SHAVED

When the binder has trimmed off the whole margin of a leaf and touched ink, but has not actually cut off more than the outer edge of any printed letters, the result is indicated by such terms as 'HEADLINES slightly shaved', 'some SIDE-NOTES shaved', or 'CATCHWORDS shaved on pages 16–20'. He has grazed the text and drawn blood; and it is proper that the synonym for *shaved*, in this context, should be *touched*; but it is hardly a wound, which would justify *text cut into*, or *cropped*.

SHEEP

A soft leather, with little grain. Good sheepskin, well handled (as it was in Germany around 1800), can make a not despicable binding. It was a popular TRADE BINDING for 17th century verse and other small books. But it has mostly been used for the commoner and cheaper sort of work; and it is all too liable to loss of surface on the covers, weakness at the joints and tearing off in long strips.

SHEET

The sheet is essentially a printer's unit. The type for two pages (for a folio), four (for a quarto), eight (for an octavo), is set up, and then printed off on one side of the sheet. The sheet is then 'perfected' by printing off an equivalent number of pages on its other side. (See also FORME.) The result is folded into a quire (or section or GATHERING), and assembled into sequence with its fellows for sewing and binding (or casing); but these operations are performed not by the printer but in the bindery.

The description above, based on hand-press procedure and valid for most books printed before the late 19th century, does not apply to the enormous sheets manufactured for modern high-speed presses, nor, *a fortiori*, to rotary printing from a continuous reel of paper (a bibliographical nightmare).

SHELF-MARK

See PRESS-MARK.

SHORT COPY

This is a shoulder-note

A copy whose margins have been severely cut down by the binder.

SHORT-TITLE

Originally the abbreviated title by which an Act of Parliament is officially designated, *short-title* is used in the same sense for books; e.g. *short-title list, short-title catalogue*, which mean that only so much of the title is given as to ensure recognition.

SHORT-TITLE CATALOGUE (STC)

A Short-Title Catalogue of Books printed in England Scotland and Ireland and of English books printed abroad 1475–1640. Compiled by A. W. Pollard and G. R. Redgrave (with the help of others). London, The Bibliographical Society, 1926.

STC, a landmark in enumerative bibliography and one of the most frequently quoted of reference books, has been several times reissued. A revised edition is in preparation.

SHOULDER-NOTES

Notes printed in the outer margin at the top of the page.

SIDE-NOTES

This is a side-note

Notes printed in the outer margin alongside the text to which they refer. This position makes them vulnerable to the binder's knife; e.g. 'some side-notes cut into' or 'with the side-note on page 61 intact' (the implication being that it usually *is* cut into).

SIGNATURES

The letters (or, in some modern books, numerals) printed in the tail margin of the first leaf (at least) of each GATHERING or section of a book, as a guide to the binder in assembling them correctly. (*See, for instance, p.* 177 *or p.* 193 *of this book.*) Signatures normally run from A to Z, omitting, by convention, J and U, which in earlier days were capitalised as I and V, and also W. If the whole alphabet has been run through, they usually proceed to

AA, BB, or Aa, Bb, etc. These are commonly indicated in bibliographical descriptions as 2A, 2B, 3A, 3B, etc. When, as an alternative, a single-letter alphabet is simply repeated, it is convenient to indicate the subsequent alphabets as ^{2}A, ^{3}A, ^{2}B, ^{3}B, etc.

The PRELIMINARY LEAVES are sometimes not signed at all (in which case the text may begin with signature B); sometimes signed with a lower-case letter or letters; occasionally signed with an asterisk or similar symbol. The title-leaf is almost never signed; the HALF-TITLE or pre liminary BLANK is occasionally signed (especially in 16th and 17th century English books); preliminary leaves following an unsigned half-title and/or title are frequently signed A3 or A2, etc.

(N.B.—The above generalisations are valid only for English books. American printers have commonly used all 26 letters of the alphabet. But since Mr. Jacob Blanck tells us that 'not infrequently 19th century American books bore not one but two or more sets of signature marks; occasionally none applies to the folding', we must accept, with however heavy a sigh, his conclusion that 'no general rule for the expression of signature marks may be applied to American books'.)

Signature is also used, by extension, to mean the gathering or section itself; e.g. 'last signature stained', or 'two signatures missing', or 'lacks first leaf of sig. F'.

For the bibliographical description of unsigned leaves and gatherings, see COLLATION.

SIGNED BINDINGS

The binder's name will usually be given in a catalogue description if the binding is of any quality or interest, and if its executant or designer can be identified. E.g. 'in a handsome red morocco binding by Kalthoeber', or 'half levant, gilt tops, by Zaehnsdorf'.

Bindings can be *positively* attributed on several kinds of evidence: (1) In early bindings, by initials, cypher or name impressed in BLIND on the outside of the covers, whether by a single TOOL or incorporated in a ROLL or PANEL. (2) By a printed or engraved label, known as a

BINDER'S TICKET: normally pasted on to the upper corner of one of the front endpapers, but very occasionally at the foot of the title-page. Introduced in the 1720's, binders' tickets were widely used from 1780 onwards both in England and France, but the practice declined sharply after the 1830's. (3) By the binder's name (rarely initials) stamped on the inside edge of the front or back cover; or, by many French and a very few English binders of the late 18th and early 19th centuries, at the foot of the spine; or, rarely, along the fore or lower edge of the front cover; or, by Henry Walther if no one else, along the inside front hinge; or, from the second quarter of the 19th century onwards, in ink at the edge of one of the ENDPAPERS. These signatures are nowadays often done with a name-PALLET. (4) By a manuscript note of the owner for whom it was bound. (5) Occasionally by some external evidence, such as the binder's bill or a reference in correspondence.

Often, however, no such evidence is available; and then the cataloguer must fall back on an *inferential* attribution, based too often only on stylistic grounds. This is generally a much more hazardous exercise than he supposes, since at any date binders in any given locality have used the same materials and brazenly copied each other's designs. With an early, rare or important binding, such an attribution will often, it is true, be buttressed by references to the use of the same individual ornaments on other bindings which can be positively assigned to a particular binder. But outside this still not fully documented area, the degree of credence to be accorded to such an attribution must depend on one's confidence in the person who makes it: confidence first in his knowledge and judgment; secondly in his integrity. An expert, appraising a binding characteristic of the style and workmanship of a well-known binder, may think he can be sure that it is, or is not, by (say) Staggemeier or Hering; yet the expert does not live who can tell some late Bedfords from early Rivières. And certainly many more bindings have been optimistically assigned to Derome or Padeloup, Mearne, Edwards or Roger Payne, than ever came out of their shops.

The prudent collector, therefore, when confronted with any binding attribution in an auctioneer's or bookseller's catalogue, will look first to see whether it is positive or inferential. And if it is the latter, he will take thought whether Mr. X is or is not apt to know what he is about in such matters. Signed bindings by admired craftsmen command, of course, a higher price than unsigned ones, however confidently attributed; but a confident attribution (whether well or ill founded) is usually considered by him who advances it to justify a higher price than would the more cautious description 'in the style of' or 'in the manner of'. Any experienced collector who even contemplates ordering a book chiefly remarkable for its binding otherwise than on approval is wont to scrutinise very carefully the evidence for any attribution attached to it. And even when he has it before him, he remembers that, although it is difficult to imitate or tamper with a name-pallet, unscrupulous persons have been known to transfer a binder's ticket from a dull or damaged example of some master's work to a handsome or interesting book bound in his manner but unfortunately (or fortunately) unsigned.

PUBLISHER'S CLOTH bindings between 1835 and 1850 occasionally had the binder's name stamped on their sides, usually somewhere in the border. And an artist's name (e.g. Gustave Doré, Aubrey Beardsley) or monogram (e.g. J[ohn] L[eighton]) is sometimes to be seen on carefully designed books of the second half of the century.

SILKED

When the leaves of a book are so fragile and/or have required so much repair that they have been faced on both sides with some thin, transparent textile or plastic fabric, they are said to be *silked*.

SINGLETON

A jargon word (of recent origin in this sense) meaning a single leaf, where a CONJUGATE pair would be expected in a COLLATION. A singleton will either be the surviving leaf where the other has been severed for insertion elsewhere, or the severed half itself in its inset position, or an extra leaf printed separately, probably at the last minute.

SIXTIES BOOKS

This label has become of late years a not infrequent subject-heading in booksellers' catalogues. Applying strictly to the published products of the English illustrators of the 1860's (particularly of the Pre-Raphaelite group), as popularised by the pioneer studies of Gleeson White and Forrest Reid, it is apt to include such immediate chronological predecessors as Moxon's illustrated edition of Tennyson *Poems* 1857 and reprints or late-comers from the succeeding decades. Many of such volumes were put out in elaborately decorated bindings with gilt-edged leaves and often BEVELLED EDGES (sometimes called *table books*), and they were frequently cased by the GUTTA-PERCHA technique rather than sewn, so that they are hard to find in sound condition.

SIZE, SIZED, RE-SIZED

Size is a glutinous or viscid wash used in the preparation of certain kinds of paper (as well as other substances). And the collector is only concerned with it in one context. When a leaf or leaves of a book have been WASHED, to remove dirt, writing, etc., the chemical detergents are apt to remove the sizing from the paper, leaving it limp and weak. A washed leaf or gathering, therefore, is likely to be also re-sized, and therefore one further degree removed from its original state.

SIZE OF BOOKS
See FORMAT.

SIZES OF TYPE
See POINT SYSTEM, TYPE MEASUREMENT.

SKIVER

The humblest of all forms of leather used for book-binding. It is very thin, being split from the inner side of a sheepskin and tanned in sumach. When rubbed, worn or scarred (as often), it is hard to tell from ROAN; nor is the distinction of much importance, for both are despised.

SLIP

Any piece of printed paper of an area substantially less than the page of the book, etc., with which it is connected; whether physically, e.g. pasted-on CANCEL slips, TIPPED-IN ERRATA slips or ADVERTISEMENT slips; or by loose insertion, e.g. PRESENTATION slips, REVIEW slips.

SLIP CASE

See CASES AND BOXES.

SOLANDER CASE

Originally invented by Daniel Charles Solander (1736–82), a pupil of Linnæus, for the preservation of botanical specimens in the British Museum, where he was an assistant librarian. Subsequently adopted for housing prints, and in due course books also. The solander is strictly a box, of the fall-down-back or fall-down-front type, rather than a case (see CASES AND BOXES). In its full-dress form, whether of full or half leather, it has a rounded back, projecting SQUARES like a book, and a spring catch or catches.

SOPHISTICATED

This adjective, as applied to a book, is simply a polite synonym for DOCTORED or faked-up. It would be equally appropriate to a second edition in which a first edition title-leaf had been inserted, to another from which the words *second edition* had been carefully erased, to a first edition RE-CASED in second edition covers, to a copy whose half-title had been supplied from another copy (MADE-UP) or another edition or was in FACSIMILE.

It is therefore naturally a term very rarely found in a catalogue description except in its negative form, *unsophisticated*; e.g. 'a somewhat shaken but entirely unsophisticated copy of this rare book'. First noted use, 1790.

SOUND COPY

This means what it says and no more, for if the copy were a fine one, the cataloguer would say so.

SPANISH CALF

A method, originating in Spain, of decorating the sides of a CALF binding by bold dashes, or large flecks, of red and green acid dye.

SPINE

That part of a book which is visible as it stands closed on the shelf; not uncommonly called in antiquarian parlance the *backstrip*, and sometimes the *back*. The last comes naturally in such phrases as *smooth back*, *panelled back*, *gilt back* and others descriptive of leather bindings, but it is to be avoided in those contexts in which it could be confused with the back (or lower) cover.

SPRINKLED

Used (1) of calf bindings and (2) of the edges of leaves, and meaning coloured with small specks or spots. In sprinkled (or speckled) calf, these are normally of a darker brown than the natural leather (stained calf is very rarely sprinkled). For edges the commonest colour is a dull red. Many, perhaps most, books bound in calf or sheep before about 1850 had their edges sprinkled. In recent times the technique has been mainly restricted to reference books, technical books, library rebindings and the like.

SQUARE

A technical term in binding, meaning the inside edge of the covers which projects beyond the leaves of the book.

SQUARE BRACKETS

These are used for enclosing an author's or publisher's name, the place or date of publication, or any other detail in the description of a book or manuscript which is supplied, not from the object described, but from an external source; e.g. Beckford's name as the author of the anonymous *Vathek*, or '[London, *circa* 1890]' for the edition of Mrs. Browning's *Sonnets from the Portuguese* allegedly printed at Reading in 1847.

STABBED, STAB-HOLES

The GATHERINGS (or sections or quires) of most books are sewn up the centre of the fold. But very thin books, pamphlets, magazines or PART-ISSUES would sometimes be sewn through sideways, when they are said to be *stabbed*, from the holes stabbed through the leaves to receive the thread. (The modern term for this is *side-stitched*.)

The existence of 'the original stab-holes' will sometimes be cited as evidence that a bound or cased copy of a part-issued book was bound from the parts, which were usually stabbed, and was not a copy of the subsequent volume-issue for which the quires would have been stitched in the ordinary way (see PART-ISSUED BOOKS IN VOLUME FORM).

STAMP, STAMPED

(1) See BOOK-STAMP, REVIEW COPIES.

(2) A term not used by professional binders which has nevertheless established itself in descriptions of book bindings. It is best limited to the engraved design on a BLOCK, or the impression of a block on the covers of a book, as distinct from decoration executed by a wheel-tool or cut in the leather. Examples are: PANEL-STAMPS, ARMORIAL stamps, and those large centre and corner stamps used in the second half of the 16th century and the first half of the 17th which must have been blocked in a press.

STAPLED

Wire staples as a substitute for stitching seem to have been introduced for publisher's binding about 1880; but, apart from their tendency to rust, they have never been satisfactory for cloth-bound books. They have, however, continued to be used to hold together pamphlets, magazines, etc., for issue either wrapped or without covers.

STATE

(1) Of illustrations, frontispieces, engraved titles, etc., which may show evidence of wear, alteration, re-engraving in whole or in part, or which may have been produced in alternative forms; e.g. of *Gulliver's Travels* 1726, 'a fine

STATE (continued)

copy with the portrait in the first state, without Gulliver's name round the oval'; of *The Pickwick Papers* 1836–37, 'the plate in Part 12 is in the earliest state, before the addition of the hat on the front bench'; of Thornton *Temple of Flora* 1799–1807, 'an exceptional copy with the plates in two states, plain and coloured'.

(2) Of the printed text: see ISSUES AND STATES.

(3) Of the individual copy: 'in fine state' (see CONDITION) or 'rarely seen in ORIGINAL STATE'.

STATUTORY COPIES
See COPYRIGHT LIBRARIES

STEREOTYPE

'The method or process of printing in which a solid plate of type-metal, cast from a papier-mâché or plaster mould taken from the surface of a FORME of type, is used for printing from, instead of the forme itself' (SOED).

Invented by Johann Muller of Leyden in the first decade of the 18th century, re-invented by William Ged of Edinburgh in the late 1720's, re-invented again by Alexander Tilloch of Glasgow about 1780, and practically commercialised by Earl Stanhope's process soon after 1800, this technique was widely used in England and (particularly) America from the second decade of the 19th century onwards.

STILTED

A binder's term, meaning that the SQUARE, or projection of the covers beyond the edges of the leaves, is unusually deep. Stilting is deliberately used when a book is being bound to range on the shelf with taller neighbours. (Pepys preferred platforms for the smaller ones to stand on.) It is sometimes a pointer to REMBOÎTAGE—the putting of one book into an old binding stripped from another of not quite the same size. Amateurishly RE-CASED cloth books may also look a little stilted if the top edges of the leaves have been drastically rubbed clean, and PART-ISSUED books were sometimes stilted when cased by a local binder over-zealous with the shears.

STIPPLED

Dotted: of engravings and occasionally of the decoration of bindings.

STITCHED

See SEWN.

STRAIGHT-GRAIN MOROCCO

MOROCCO leather so treated (in the piece, not on the book) as to give it an artificial pattern, or graining, of roughly parallel lines. The technique, said by French historians to be an English invention, dates from the second half of the 18th century.

STUB

A stub is the narrow—sometimes very narrow—strip of a leaf remaining after it has been severed from its counterpart (or CONJUGATE leaf), usually before the book was sewn. When detected—and in a firmly bound book even a naked stub is easily overlooked—it acts (or should act) as an emphatic red light. For it immediately provokes the questions, what was here and why was it cut away?

Some stubs are innocent enough. A frontispiece, plates printed separately from the text, a last-minute additional leaf—any of these would often be provided with a deliberate small overlap, or stub, so that they could be properly stitched in with the GATHERING or section to which they belong. But any stub whose purpose is not thus easily explained, and, above all, any stub *on to which a substitute leaf has been pasted* (the hardest kind to detect), indicates a CANCEL, and therefore calls for the most diligent scrutiny.

SUBSCRIBERS, ON SUBSCRIPTION

In the 17th, 18th and early 19th centuries (and much less frequently since) expensive books, privately printed books, special copies (e.g. on LARGE PAPER or with PROOF plates) or even the whole edition would sometimes be issued *on subscription*. Subscribers who responded to the preliminary *proposal* might be asked to pay part of the price in advance, perhaps against a smaller total than that ruling after publication day. And in many cases their names would be printed, in a *list of subscribers*; hence, such catalogue notes as 'complete with the list of subscribers', or 'fine copy, but lacks the subscribers', or 'a subscriber's copy, with signature of Cardinal d'Armagnac ("two copies on imperial paper")'.

SUB-TITLE

A subordinate, usually explanatory title, additional to the main title and normally printed immediately below it. To be distinguished from HALF-TITLE and FLY-TITLE.

SUPPRESSED

(1) A *passage* may be suppressed from a book (*a*) between printings; e.g. 'Bryce *American Commonwealth* 1888, First edition, with the suppressed chapter on the Tweed Ring', meaning that this chapter appears in the first but not in the second or subsequent editions; (*b*) after publication, but while stock of the edition remains, by means of a CAN-CELLED leaf or leaves, so that copies issued earliest have the original version, while those issued later have the amended; e.g. 'Surtees *Handley Cross* 1854, First illustrated edition, first ISSUE with Leech's name mentioned in the preface'; (*c*) before publication, again by cancellation, which, if copies with the suppressed passage should by chance have survived, produces, e.g. 'Boswell *Life of Johnson* 1791, First edition, with the first STATE of Qq3 in vol. II (cancelled before publication), containing the celebrated passage on conjugal infidelity'.

(2) A *book* may be suppressed, either before publication e.g. *Alice's Adventures in Wonderland* 1865 or after e.g. Helvetius *De l'Esprit* 1758. If before, the number of copies which accidentally survived or were deliberately preserved may well have been small; sometimes very small indeed, if none had been distributed to friends of the author or prospective reviewers; often not so small as might be supposed, if advance copies had gone out or if the last-minute recall of copies already distributed to the book-sellers was ineffective.

Of books suppressed or withdrawn from circulation at a later stage, whether for legal, political or sectarian reasons, or on the instructions of a belatedly ashamed author, the

degree of subsequent rarity will depend mainly on the
number distributed before suppression. And in appraising
such notes as 'suppressed by the author and very rare' or
'the book was ordered to be burned by the public hangman',
it is well to remember that of a popular or sensational book
a large number of copies could have been distributed even
if it was suppressed very shortly after publication (e.g.
Galileo *Dialogo* 1632); whereas suppression or with-
drawal from sale of an unsuccessful volume of poems ten
or twenty years after publication probably made almost no
difference to the number available to collectors fifty years
later (e.g. Matthew Arnold *The Strayed Reveller* 1849 or
Robert Bridges *Poems* 1873).

TAIL
The lower margin of the leaf; or, in another context, the
foot of the backstrip.

TAIL-PIECE
An ornament for a blank space in the lower part of a page,
usually at the end of a chapter or poem.

TALL COPY
A copy whose head and tail margins have been only lightly
trimmed by the binder.

THICK PAPER COPY
See FINE PAPER COPY.

THOUSAND
It has been the occasional practice of some publishers during
the past hundred years to indicate the sequence of reprints,
new impressions, or new editions, not in the conventional
manner (by saying *Third Edition* on the title-page or by a
bibliographical notice on its reverse), but by a statement,
usually on the title-page, of the number of thousands
printed to date. The legend *Twelfth Thousand* (for instance)
does not disclose whether the copy which carries it is of
the second or the twelfth impression (or even edition),
unless we happen to know how many copies of each were

THOUSANDS (continued)

printed. What it does make clear is that, even though the
date below be that of the first edition and there be no
formal notice of what edition or impression this belongs to,
it is *not* a copy of the first.

See also EDITION AND IMPRESSION.

THREE-DECKER

A book in three volumes: scarcely ever used except of 19th
century novels. (A critic once described the present writer
as 'the kind of man to whom *a three-decker* means neither a
ship of the line nor a sandwich'.)

THREE-QUARTER BOUND

As HALF BOUND, but with wider leather back and corners.

TICKET

See BINDER'S TICKET

TIES

Tapes or ribbons, usually in pairs, slotted into the sides or
a binding close to the outer edge, and intended, when tied,
to prevent the covers warping or gaping. They must have
been common on vellum-bound, and not uncommon on
leather-bound, books of the 15th, 16th and early 17th
centuries, to judge by the incidence of the slots in which
they had once been set; but the survival of original ties
intact is naturally infrequent. Modern substitutes for lost
originals are generally fairly easy to detect.

Ties seem to have died out about the middle of the 17th
century, though there have been archaistic revivals, chiefly
among PRIVATE PRESSES and in other self-conscious
quarters.

TIPPED IN

Lightly attached, by gum or paste, usually at the inner
edge. Plates, ERRATA slips or a single inserted leaf will
sometimes be described as being tipped in, as distinct from
being sewn in. But the term is much more frequently used

of something originally alien to the book, which has been put with it by an earlier owner; e.g. an autograph letter from the author, or some similar associated document.

TISSUES

Tissue paper tipped in or loosely inserted opposite illustrations; originally to absorb OFFSET, later sometimes for protection (or for ostentation). Unless this tissue has, as occasionally in modern books, a caption or other printing on it, most collectors regard its presence or absence with equanimity, once its original purpose of absorbing offset or damp has been discharged.

TITLE

(1) Used loosely for either the title-*leaf* (e.g. 'the title is a CANCEL', 'title extended') or the title-*page* (e.g. 'signature on title', 'first state of the title').

(2) A book: in such contexts only as 'first edition of this popular title', or '*Under Two Flags* is the rarest Ouida title'.

TOOL, TOOLING

In binder's terminology tools are the engraved metal implements (usually of brass) with wooden handles, which are used *by hand* to impress a design on the covers of a book: ROLLS, FILLETS, PALLETS, gouges and single decorative units. The term is also used for the impressions of these implements.

Tooling should be distinguished from BLOCKING, which involves the use of a press. When tooling is carried out in BLIND, the tools are used directly on the leather and the pattern shows up merely as a darkened depression in the surface. In gold tooling the heated implement is applied through gold leaf and the pattern remains in gold.

TOP EDGES GILT
See GILT TOPS

TOUCHED
See SHAVED

195

During the years before EDITION-BINDING and PUB-
LISHER'S CLOTH—the whole period, that is, between
Johann Gutenberg, 1450, and William Pickering, 1823—
books were normally issued to the public, across the
counter, in alternative dress and at alternative prices:
(1) unbound, in folded QUIRES (latterly stitched and with
the intentionally temporary protection of WRAPPERS or
paper-covered BOARDS) for binding to the purchaser's
taste, at his order and expense, as on the Continent to this
day; or (2) at a higher price in some usually simple binding
put on by or for the bookseller.

Copies which for one reason or another never got bound
survive in boards or wrappers, or unprotected by either,
i.e. SEWN, STABBED or simply FOLDED. These survivals
are often, though not always, bibliographically interesting;
they may be significant to technical specialists; they are by
their nature uncommon; and their fragility commands
respect. But their claim to be in original state is the claim
of the embryo, and the esteem in which they have come to
be held by some collectors is excessive. For the analogy
between a boarded book of 1750 and an 1850 book in publisher's cloth is a false analogy.

The collector who is willing to clear his mind of cant on
this point would admit that when he demands the original
binding on a book (as opposed to a handsome, harmonious
or associative binding), he really means *original binding as
issued to the public*. Books that were sold unbound—
pamphlets, single plays and other slender volumes—
cannot by their nature qualify for this condition. The only
books which can qualify are those bound before sale by
the retail or wholesale bookseller: in limp VELLUM,
PARCHMENT, SHEEP or CALF in earlier times, in the 18th
century usually in calf or half calf. These are conveniently
called *trade bindings*, and they are the bibliographical
equivalent of the publisher's cloth bindings of the past
century and a half.

The trouble is that such bindings are always difficult
and often impossible to identify with absolute certainty.
Experienced collectors can do so with some confidence

perhaps three times out of five; but neither they nor an equally experienced bookseller can *prove* it oftener than perhaps once in fifty times to someone who is either ignorant or sceptical (or both). For while trade bindings have clearly marked styles in different periods and strong family likenesses at any given period, they could never be absolutely uniform, in the sense that edition-binding is uniform. Consequently, no hard-and-fast norm can be laid down for any given book; and as collectors unfortunately prefer absolute, categorical descriptions, to which a given copy manifestly does or does not conform, the obscurantist and the timid among them continue to regard the classification *trade binding* with some suspicion.

See also CONTEMPORARY, ORIGINAL STATE, EDITION-BINDING.

TRANSCRIPT

Whether it is in the author's or a copyist's hand, or type-written, a transcript implies the copying of something already completed: often, indeed, of something already published. When, for example, a poet writes out a favourite poem for a friend or an admirer, the result (although it is in his AUTOGRAPH) is a transcript, and not an original manuscript in the strict sense.

TREE CALF

A calf binding (popular in the 19th century, less common today), the sides of which have been stained by the inter-action of copperas and pearl-ash to a design resembling the graining of wood (or certain types of veneer on furniture) and then highly polished. Unless the covers are thoroughly washed at once, the copperas eats into the leather, and this accounts for the bad condition in which much tree calf is now found. The style is said to have originated in the third quarter of the 18th century and to have been popularised by John Baumgarten of London.

TRIAL BINDING

Since the early days of PUBLISHER'S CLOTH, it has been the practice of the binder to submit to the publisher (and, occasionally, the publisher to the author) samples of the cover proposed for a book. There may be alternatives of colour, of fabric, less often of lettering and decoration. For most modern books these samples are 'dummies' (i.e. mainly, if not entirely, made up of blank leaves); but in the 19th century, when production schedules were not so tight, it seems certain that finished copies were often used. For examples have occasionally survived of books normal as to their interior, whose binding differs in plausible particulars (e.g. only in colour) from that of the published edition *and* which derive from a plausible source (e.g. a member of the publisher's staff). There are even instances where it seems that a thrifty publisher used up the trial-bound copies for fulfilling his obligation to the COPYRIGHT LIBRARIES or for the author's complimentary half-dozen.

The word *seem* has been used advisedly in the preceding paragraph, because evidence of general practice is sketchy and evidence for particular books hard to come by. Thoroughly documented or even convincingly probable examples of trial binding are naturally prized by collectors: representative examples are Trollope *Marion Fay* 1882, Meredith *One of Our Conquerors* 1894, Katherine Mansfield *The Garden Party* 1922. But (no doubt for that very reason) the term is freely misapplied: to unexplained freaks, which are commoner than might be supposed; to normal but unrecorded colour-variants; occasionally, to a superior style of BINDER'S CLOTH (i.e. not publisher's binding at all); and, perhaps most commonly, to a variant or SECONDARY binding which the cataloguer happens never to have seen before.

TRIAL ISSUE or EDITION

It is known that a few authors sometimes had their work set up in type at an early stage, and a few copies printed off for circulation amongst critical friends or even for their own convenience in revision. Tennyson was one, and Bridges *The Testament of Beauty* 1927–29 is a more recent example. This practice produces a *trial edition* if the book was subsequently reset before being printed for publication; a *trial issue* if it was not, but if nevertheless the purpose, format and other circumstances of the preliminary printing were such as to distinguish the results indisputably from PROOF COPIES.

This latter distinction is not always an easy one to establish, and it is often shirked by those who suffer from, or pander to, THE CHRONOLOGICAL OBSESSION. But it is crucial to any accurate employment of the word *trial*.

TRIMMED

According to some authorities, *cut* means that the edges of a book's leaves have been cut smooth; *trimmed*, that they have been more roughly levelled. Unfortunately this convenient distinction is regularly observed neither by printers nor by the cataloguers of antiquarian books, so that in effect *trimmed* and *cut* are for our purpose almost synonymous. The term *rough-trimmed* is sometimes used for edges not cut smooth. (See UNCUT, CUT.)

TURKEY LEATHER

Leather prepared from goatskin, used very occasionally by English binders of the 16th century but not common before 1650, called *Turkey* from its country of origin. When in 1721 Lord Oxford (see HARLEIAN STYLE) imported leather from Fez, his binder distinguished between *Turkey* and MOROCCO in his bills. The latter was of inferior quality, with a grain rather like SHEEP.

TYPE FACSIMILE

A reprint which approximates to, without exactly imitating (nor with any intent to deceive), the typographical style of the original edition.

TYPE MEASUREMENT

The terminology of types and their sizes since the 16th century was evolved by type-founders and printers. But for early printed books in general and INCUNABULA in particular the bibliographers had to invent their own. They express the size of the type in a particular book by the depth of an arbitrary unit, 20 lines: thus 78R means that the book is printed in a roman type, twenty lines of which (*as in the present volume*) measure 78 millimetres in depth.

For modern terminology see POINT SIZES.

TYPE SPECIMEN

A sheet, booklet or piece of demonstration printing designed to display the various 'sorts' and sizes of a fount or founts of type, sometimes accompanied by printer's ornaments. Type specimens may be issued either by the type-founder (aimed mainly at printers, who buy type), or by the printer (aimed at publishers and others who buy printing).

TYPESCRIPT

The terminology for describing typescripts of an author's work (and many nowadays work direct on to the type-writer) has not yet been settled. The word *auto-typescript*, sometimes used to distinguish the author's typing from that of a professional copyist, is philologically barbarous and must be resisted.

There are at least three kinds of typescript to be distinguished, each of which may (and the first two of which almost certainly will) carry additions or corrections from the author's pen. They are (*a*) *Author's original typescript*: the equivalent of the original MS, or first autograph draft. (*b*) *Author's fair copy typescript*: the equivalent, executed by his own fingers, of an autograph MS fair copy. (*c*) *Copyist's typescript*: a fair copy executed by another pair of hands.

Typescript is conveniently abbreviated to TS.

UNAUTHORISED EDITION
See AUTHORISED EDITION, PIRACY

UNBOUND

This properly means that the book or pamphlet described never had covers; whether by intention, in which case the cataloguer will probably add *as issued*, or by accident. But it is still sometimes used of a volume which was once in a binding but now is not, i.e. DISBOUND. See also SEWN.

UNCUT, CUT
(OF EDGES)

Uncut is probably the most overworked word in the cataloguer's vocabulary, and it has come to exert a mesmeric—and not entirely healthy—effect on the novice collector. He will not, of course, share the delusion which provides such ready (but blank) ammunition to outsiders hostile to bibliophily, viz. that uncut is the same thing as unopened, with the corollary that collectors prefer their books not only unread but unreadable. For UNOPENED means that the leaves have not been severed by the paper-knife from their neighbours. But unless the functional significance of uncut edges is properly understood, a rational preference for them *in their place* can all too easily degenerate into DECKLE-FETISHISM.

Collectors have always, and rightly, cherished copies with ample margins; for it has been the habit of binders from earliest times to trim off more rather than less of the rough edges of the leaves than was intended by those who designed the printed page; and every time a book is re-bound it is liable to lose more. Of books published before the age of EDITION-BINDING, therefore, a tall copy is preferable (other things being equal) to a short one. Yet the edges of all these books were intended to be cut smooth, even if they were not thereafter gilded, MARBLED, SPRINKLED, GAUFFRED or stained with colour. Any copy of such a book, therefore, which has survived with its edges entirely uncut is an accident, a specimen of the embryo stage in book production: rare no doubt, bibliographically interesting sometimes, but not representative of the book as intended for the reader's shelf. (See also TRADE BINDING.)

With the adoption (1830–40) of PUBLISHER'S CLOTH as the original and intentionally permanent covering of the majority of books published in England and America, the collector's attitude to their edges is radically changed. For if he is in pursuit, as he usually is, of a copy in its original condition as issued to the public, he will require that its edges (whether uncut, rough-trimmed or cut smooth) shall conform to a now standardised margin. All that he needs, therefore, in this particular respect, is an assurance that the edges have not been *cut down* by a re-binder or repairer. And a good deal of space is saved by those book-sellers who make it plain at the beginning of their catalogues that all books described as being in original cloth have their edges as issued, and so need not constantly repeat the word *uncut*.

See also CONDITION, DECKLE EDGES, TRIMMED.

UNIQUE

A manuscript or an autograph letter or a drawing is *ipso facto* unique. A book with an inscription or annotations is reasonably described as unique in respect of such additions, since the author or other inscriber is hardly likely to have repeated them, identically, in another and exactly similar copy of the same edition. But very few books can in themselves be called unique. And much scrupulous documentation is required to substantiate even the tentative description *apparently unique*.

UNKNOWN TO . . . or NOT IN . . .

Few things are more agreeable, whether to collector or bookseller, than the discovery that one possesses a book which the accredited experts have overlooked or failed to recognise for what it is. But the cataloguer's cry of joy must not be allowed to deafen us to the voice of reason; and this enjoins us to ask (1) whether the authority thus negatively cited is a good one, (2) whether the scope and nature of the work of reference are strictly relevant, and (3) whether possibly the book is, in fact, listed in it, but under some less than obvious heading.

It is easy enough to score off an out-of-date author-bibliography or a notoriously incompetent bibliographer. It is not fair to saddle a general survey with an unclaimed obligation to list every minor production, and then trumpet up something it does not mention. It is often difficult to be sure that, for instance, an anonymous devotional compilation is not, somewhere, in STC. And while it would be legitimate to boast of an Elizabethan play *not in Greg* or a first edition of Trollope *unknown to Sadleir*, it does not mean much that a book is *not mentioned in DNB*.

UNLETTERED

Without any title or author's name on the spine of the binding. Until about 1600 many, if not most, books which were titled outside at all were lettered in ink or paint on the fore-edges of the leaves; for they stood or lay on the shelf with their backs to the wall. And the binder's habit of omitting the title from the spine (not unconnected perhaps with the cost of gold leaf) persisted long after the change to the modern arrangement. Even on bespoke bindings, lettering-pieces (leather labels) were rare in England before about 1660, so that unlettered bindings on books of the 16th and first half of the 17th centuries are normal. Often the owner will have titled the book in ink, whether on a paper label or directly on to the vellum or leather; but when gilt lettering (direct or on labels) is found on such books, it will usually have been added later.

Unlettered (though sometimes volume-numbered) calf and sheep may be found in the cheaper styles of binding— that is, bookseller's or TRADE BINDINGS—till late in the 18th century.

Unlettered (i.e. unlabelled) paper spines were the rule for BOARDED books till the 1780's, became steadily less common till about 1810, and must thereafter have been exceptional. Paper spines untitled but volume-numbered with an ink stamp are occasionally seen. And many, of course, have MS titling in ink, though whether in a particular example this was added by the bookseller or the purchaser is anybody's guess.

UNOPENED

This means that the leaves of a book issued entirely untrimmed (and therefore having the folding of its component sections still intact at the top and fore-edges) have not been severed from their neighbours with the paper-knife. It must not be confused, as it often is by philistines, with UNCUT.

UNPRESSED

Strictly speaking, this means that the book of which it is used has never been in the binder's press, so that the paper preserves its original briskness of texture. But the term is often applied loosely to bound books in which this pleasing quality has survived: a sense already quite adequately served by the word CRISP.

UNRECORDED

A truly Olympian term in the hierarchy of rarity, when properly and responsibly used of a book which in the nature of things ought to have been recorded. But the less important the book, the greater the chance of its existence having passed unnoticed in later centuries and the less the significance of the omission.

See also UNKNOWN TO ...

UNSEWN, UNSTITCHED
See FOLDED

UNSOPHISTICATED

Pure, genuine, unrestored. (See SOPHISTICATED.)

USED COPY

Pretty bad; about level with a READING COPY, but probably not so far gone as a WORKING COPY.

VARIANT

A general-purpose term used to describe a copy or copies of an EDITION exhibiting some variation, whether of text, title-page, illustrations, paper or binding, from another copy or copies of the same edition. Its use does not necessarily imply that the copy or copies in question are abnormal; in fact, it is most frequently and properly used when doubts exist as to the priority, or even the precise relationship, between the two or more observed variants, and where in consequence no norm has been established. As Greg once put it: 'I have treated bibliographical variants as essentially unordered'.

Thus, to describe a copy as being 'a variant of Shandygaff's first ISSUE', or 'in a variant binding of blue cloth (normal copies being in red)', is much more prudent and sensible than rash talk about 'earliest issue, unknown to Shandygaff' or 'trial binding, probably unique' (see ISSUE-MONGERS).

VARIOUS DATES, YEARS (v.d., v.y.)

Used in the description (*a*) of a volume containing several works of different date, and (*b*) of a work consisting of several volumes of different date.

VELLUM

The skin of a calf, not tanned but de-greased and specially treated, used either for writing or printing on, or in binding. Vellum is nowadays sometimes made from lambskin or goatskin (and even, Mr. Kenneth Hobson avers, from rabbit). *Uterine* vellum, a term sometimes found in the description of a manuscript, was made, in the 13th and 14th centuries, from the skin of an unborn or still-born animal.

Most medieval manuscripts, whether ILLUMINATED or not, were written on vellum. And from the first book (the 42-line *Bible* of *c.* 1455) onwards—though rarely between 1520 and 1780—it has been the occasional practice of printers and publishers of books of some typographical pretensions to print a few copies on vellum.

For binding, limp vellum or limp PARCHMENT was commonly used in the 16th and 17th centuries, sometimes PANELLED in gilt, but often quite plain. In later centuries vellum has more commonly been used like leather; that is, as covering (or half or quarter covering) for board sides. Green vellum was used occasionally in the 17th, more extensively in the 18th, century; though except for what is known as 'Newbery's manner' less often in English than in French binderies. Vellum can be stained any colour but seldom is. It is remarkably durable, but tends to warp or cockle in dry air. It is best cleaned either with a clot of damp breadcrumbs or with milk—fatal to 'art (i.e. imitation) vellum'.

VERSO

The back, or reverse, side of the LEAF; i.e. the left-hand page of an open book. Verso is the complement to recto, and these are the terms generally used in the more technical kind of bibliographical description; e.g. 'A4 recto, Dedication; verso, List of illustrations', or 'S8 verso, blank except for printer's device' (see COLLATION). They are also used whenever, even in more informal descriptions, both sides of an unpaginated leaf have to be referred to. When there is need to identify only the verso of the leaf, the synonymous term *reverse* is often used; e.g. 'the reverse of the title-leaf is blank'.

VIGNETTE

(1) A small ornamental or decorative design, used on a title-page or as a head- or tail-piece to a chapter or division of a book.

(2) Any illustration not enclosed in a border or squared off at the edges but shading away.

VOLVELLE

'A device consisting of one or more movable parchment or paper discs rotating on string pivots and surrounded by either graduated or figured circles. With its help problems concerning the calendar, tide tables, astronomy and astrology could be solved.' (H. M. Nixon)

WASHED

The French habitually wash not merely leaves but whole volumes, and cheerfully admit it: e.g. "En parfaite condition originale. Bien lavée et encollée" (RESIZED). The English and the Americans do so much less freely, and so unostentatiously that you might almost think they were ashamed of it. It is all a matter of convention. Washing with chemicals (the efficient way) takes out not only the spots, stains, writing or other blemishes, but also the SIZE from the paper, which is usually re-applied by giving the leaves a size bath. One process or the other is apt to leave a smell, and this will sometimes confirm the suspicion of a washed leaf or section if the nose is applied to the inner margins of the open book, where it is most apt to linger.

WASTE
(PRINTER'S OR BOOKSELLER'S)

Spoiled or surplus printed sheets are called *waste*. Binders have often used these in the back of a volume, for making up boards, or in earlier days for ENDPAPERS. Such waste might derive either from a printing house (PROOFS, trial sheets, overprintings) or from a bookseller (surplus quires or spoiled copies of recent books, discarded fragments of old ones). *Bookseller's waste* might have come from anywhere, and few conclusions can be automatically drawn from the presence of an identified piece of it found in a binding. But *printer's waste* was normally disposed of near by, and can often be helpful evidence for localising the binding in which it was used.

WATERMARK

A distinguishing mark or device incorporated in the wire mesh of the tray in which the pulp settles during the process of papermaking, and visible in the finished product when held against the light. The maker's name or initials, the place or date of manufacture, if added, were more apt to be embodied in the *countermark*, a subsidiary and smaller unit introduced in the 17th century, generally placed in the opposite half of the sheet to the watermark proper. The presence of a watermark is normal in LAID paper, rarely found in WOVE paper used for book printing. Watermarks provide valuable evidence of the make-up of a book; and they are often helpful pointers to the existence of a CANCEL or the cunning insertion of an alien leaf.

The pioneer of indexing watermarks was Briquet; but the whole technique of photographing, identifying and dating them is in process of revolution (begun in Leningrad and later developed by Allan Stevenson).

WHOLESALER'S BINDING

(1) An occasionally justifiable synonym for TRADE BINDING on 18th century books.

(2) A seldom confidently applicable term for the results of the practice prevalent in Regency and early Victorian times by which wholesale booksellers, especially those catering to the provincial and overseas trade, bought their stock of new books in QUIRES and had them bound in bulk, but independently of the publisher. This practice was widespread before EDITION-BINDING came in (1825–

30); but as it was commonest in the field of fiction, and as it continued to suit the wholesale novel-distributors, novels were the last class of books (of any bulk) to go over to the uniform of publisher's cloth.

Consequently, quite as much BOARDED and HALF CLOTH fiction between 1820 and 1845 (at least) was put out in wholesaler's binding as in the publisher's. The same printed labels were used, and since little account is, or can be, taken of variations in the colour of paper-covered board sides, the two are usually almost impossible to tell apart—unless the wholesaler had one of his catalogues inserted in the copies boarded to his order.

Collectors in general remain unaware of the difference. And it is perhaps as well that they should continue to dis-regard it. The quest for early Victorian three-deckers in any sort of original state is quite arduous enough as it is.

WING

Short-Title Catalogue of Books printed in England, Scotland, Ireland, Wales and British America, and of English Books printed in other Countries 1641–1700. Compiled by Donald Wing of the Yale University Library. Printed for the Index Society by Columbia University Press, New York.

Vol. I.   A–England, 1945.
Vol. II.   England–Oxwick, 1948.
Vol. III. P–Z, 1951.

A continuation to 1700 of Pollard and Redgrave's original SHORT-TITLE CATALOGUE: often (indeed much too often) cited by booksellers in support of an asseveration of rarity either on the alleged ground that the edition in question has been overlooked by Mr. Wing or (in the form 'only five copies in U.S.A. according to Wing') because his location of copies in representative American libraries is limited to five. A second edition is impending.

WIRE LINES

The close-set lines in LAID paper, made by the wire mesh in the bottom of the frame and called nowadays by paper experts *laid lines*. They are to be distinguished from the wider-spaced and heavier lines running at right angles to them, which are called CHAIN LINES.

WITH ALL FAULTS (w.a.f.)

See NOT SUBJECT TO RETURN

WOOD-CUT, WOOD-ENGRAVING

Strictly speaking, a wood-*cut* is cut with a knife along the plank, while a wood-*engraving* is cut with a graver or burin on the cross-section, usually of a piece of box-wood. The latter makes for harder wood and therefore permits a much greater delicacy in the design. But the terms are used indiscriminately by most cataloguers (and many other people) for any illustration printed from wood as distinct from metal. Both, indeed, are often used to describe illustrations which (as frequently since the 1860's) were printed from electrotype metal blocks taken from the original (but less durable) wood blocks; for it is often impossible to tell these from impressions of the original wood.

WORKING COPY

The humblest term in the vocabulary of CONDITION.

WORMHOLES

The holes made in paper, and sometimes also in the boards and leather of bindings, by bookworms—maggots of variegated species but uniformly predatory habits, particularly addicted to INCUNABULA and other precious early books printed on good nourishing rag paper. Apparently first noticed (and fearsomely illustrated) in Hooke *Micrographia* 1665, the bookworm was treated at appropriate length in *The Enemies of Books* (revised edition 1888) by William Blades, who cited no less than eight Latin names given by entomologists to one or other of its varieties. We are told by the experts that the bookworm 'cannot stand sunlight', but what does that profit us?

Worming, provided it is not in battalion strength, is considered by many collectors a less offensive blemish than dirt or browning. And since the worm normally ate steadily through the leaves, his track is occasionally useful in detecting MADE-UP copies.

WOVE PAPER

Paper with an even, granulated texture, mostly made on a continuous close-meshed wire belt. Invented about 1755, it has been the usual paper for ordinary book-printing since the early 19th century. It is distinct in its method of manufacture from LAID paper and is normally distinguishable from it by the absence of CHAIN LINES and WIRE (or laid) LINES.

Some wove papers, however, are made to look like laid paper, with imitation CHAIN LINES, etc., so it is fortunate that the collector of modern books seldom has to worry his head about the difference.

WRAPPERS, WRAPPERED

Paper covers, plain, MARBLED or printed. A wrappered book, in antiquarian parlance, is what would ordinarily be called a paper-back, and it has nothing to do with dust-wrappers or DUST-JACKETS.

In some contexts the fact that the wrappers are original is taken for granted; e.g. '*Waverley* in boards [i.e. original boards] is rarer than *Adonais* in wrappers'. But in routine catalogue descriptions this cannot be assumed unless the cataloguer says so.

Like paper boards, wrappers were used as a temporary covering for books and pamphlets during the century preceding the introduction of PUBLISHER'S CLOTH (*c.* 1825); and some discussion of this intermediate stage in book-production will be found under the entries on BOARDS, ORIGINAL STATE, TRADE BINDING.

For books published *after* uniform EDITION-BINDING became general, original wrappers are no less and no more obligatory for the discriminating collector than original cloth.

WRITING BOOKS

Manuals of CALLIGRAPHY which include a series of engraved or wood-cut specimens.

XYLOGRAPHY, XYLOGRAPHICA

See BLOCKBOOKS.

YAPP, YAPP EDGES

Yapp, so called after the London bookseller who invented it about 1860, is a style of binding (usually in leather, often limp) with overlapping edges or flaps on all three edges. Hence, *yapp edges*, meaning the flaps. The yapp style (no relation to the overlapping fore-edges of limp-vellum-bound books of the 16th and 17th centuries) is mostly used for books of devotion, slim volumes of verse printed for private circulation, 'tasteful' reprints of the *Rubá'iyát, Poems of Passion, Sonnets from the Portuguese*, etc. The American term for this style (according to *The Bookman's Glossary*) is *divinity circuit* or *circuit edges*.

YELLOW-BACK

'The nickname given to the particular type of cheap edition evolved about the middle of the last century for display and sale on railway bookstalls. It was usually (but not always) a cheap edition of fiction; it usually (but not always) cost two shillings; its basic colouring was usually (but not always) yellow' (Michael Sadleir).

[DEVICE, used as a TAIL-PIECE]

HEAD

FORE-EDGE

HINGE

[This is the FREE ENDPAPER]

TAIL